The Practice
of
Supportive
Psychotherapy

The Practice of Supportive Psychotherapy

David S. Werman, M.D.

Professor of Psychiatry

Duke University Medical Center

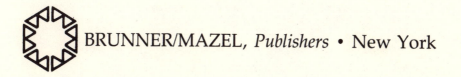
BRUNNER/MAZEL, *Publishers* • New York

Library of Congress Cataloging in Publication Data

Werman, David S., 1922-
  The practice of supportive psychotherapy.

  Bibliography: p.
  Includes index.
  1. Supportive psychotherapy. 2. Psychoanalysis.
3. Insight in psychotherapy. I. Title. [DNLM:
1. Physician-Patient Relations. 2. Psychotherapy—
methods. WM 420 W489p]
RC489.S86W47   1984   616.89'14   84-12740
ISBN 0-87630-365-3

Published by
BRUNNER/MAZEL, INC.
19 Union Square
New York, New York 10003

MANUFACTURED IN THE UNITED STATES OF AMERICA

10 9 8 7 6 5 4

To Claudia and Marco

Foreword

It is hard to believe that a topic as important and challenging as the one addressed in this book has been neglected for so long. The need for supportive psychotherapy is one of the most pressing and pervasive in our field. Yet it has been the stepchild, most often relegated to the least experienced among us, and consistently regarded as less prestigious than other modalities, especially insight-oriented psychotherapy and psychopharmacologic therapy.

This volume reflects the extensive experience of a wise and skilled clinician-educator in psychiatry and psychoanalysis. In presenting a balanced, comprehensive, detailed, nondoctrinaire, and warm human treatment of the subject, it will do much to correct previous misunderstanding and error. Dr. Werman makes it clear that, while supportive psychotherapy can and should be based on psychodynamic understanding of patients, the technical principles that guide application of such understanding in supportive treatment are quite different from those guiding insight-oriented therapy. Careful reflection upon the text and its many clinical examples will suggest that good supportive psychotherapy is extremely difficult and demanding of special skills. To be effective the therapist must be able to understand patients in depth and to apply such understanding toward the goal of helping them

The Practice of Supportive Psychotherapy

attain as much improvement in individual adjustment and comfort in life as may be possible. And it is clear that realistic perspective in appraising the patients' total life situation is required for setting realistic treatment goals that can bring gratification to the therapist, rather than the frustration that may result when unrealistic expectations are held.

Psychotherapy and psychopharmacologic therapy are not mutually exclusive alternatives. In fact they should supplement and complement each other in treatment programs. The profound changes that the newer drugs have made possible in the long-term management of chronically and intermittently ill psychiatric patients increase the need for supportive psychotherapy, especially as patients are treated for longer periods outside hospitals.

This book, better than any written material previously available, can guide the reader in learning the requisite techniques but it offers much more than that. In providing relevant theoretical rationale it promotes understanding of underlying principles and so prepares the reader for continuing growth and maturation of personal therapeutic skills and proficiency.

Psychiatric educators will welcome this book. It will make their jobs easier. Clinicians at all levels of experience will learn from it and, ultimately, vast numbers of patients will benefit from it.

Morton F. Reiser, M.D.
Charles B.G. Murphy Professor of Psychiatry
Chairman, Dept. of Psychiatry
Yale University

Preface

Although the vast majority of patients seen in psychiatric clinics and mental health centers require, and presumably are treated with, supportive psychotherapy, it is an unfortunate paradox that so little teaching is devoted to this form of treatment. It is rare to find case conferences, didactic seminars, or supervisory sessions specifically focused on this important modality of psychotherapy; typically, the subject is dealt with within the context of deciding what to do with patients who are not appropriate candidates for insight-oriented psychotherapy. What supportive psychotherapy is, for whom it is indicated, how it is carried out—these are questions that are rarely explored. Indeed, they are only infrequently asked.

However, supportive psychotherapy is not a vague alternative to insight-oriented treatment; it is a well-defined form of psychotherapy that represents a logical application of psychoanalytic concepts to a particular class of patients whose characteristics can usually be clearly identified. Too frequently, patients for whom this modality seems indicated are assigned to the least experienced members of the clinic team—medical students, psychology interns, or social work students. Their understanding of what they are supposed to do is poorly, and often not at all, understood.

The implications of such assignments are that little or no experience or knowledge is required to practice supportive psychotherapy, and that the principal task of the trainee is merely to meet regularly with the patient, be "supportive," but to work without specific goals, plan of action, or theoretical framework within which the therapy can be conceptualized. Consequently, these assignments convey an attitude which almost explicitly depreciates the practice of supportive psychotherapy. Admittedly, a therapist will sometimes intuitively work well with a patient in "supportive therapy"; too often, however, the absence of a conceptual system within which he can view his work leads to a notable lack of direction to the treatment.

At other times, one observes a therapist struggling vainly to do insight work with a patient for whom that type of treatment is not indicated. The therapist persists in making "dynamic interpretations" which have no apparent impact on the patient; on occasion, this may be useful because the interpretations inadvertently function supportively by providing the patient with intellectual defenses against anxiety which are preferable to existing, more maladaptive patterns.

The views expressed here, therefore, are based on psychoanalytic concepts. From personal experience both as a clinician practicing psychoanalysis and psychotherapy, and as a teacher and supervisor, I believe that psychoanalytic theory provides the most useful conceptual framework to guide the psychotherapist in his or her work. Whether I am engaged in practicing supportive or insight-oriented psychotherapy, I have found psychoanalytic theory both intellectually satisfying and as possessing a high explanatory power.

I have not attempted systematically to review the literature, limited as it is, that relates to supportive psychotherapy, nor have I consistently attempted to mention views that differ from those I am advancing. By design, this book conveys those aspects of my clinical experience, as well as those of colleagues and students, which I have found to be useful. I hope that other therapists who have views different from those presented in the following pages will be stimulated to put them forward and develop them. In that way, interest in supportive psychotherapy and its teaching will be encouraged.

The plan of this book is first to present the reader with broad concepts of a theoretical and strategic nature and then to focus on more specific tactical issues. Inevitably, the two approaches are not fully separable. I have generally sought to avoid jargon; when I use certain technical terms or phrases, I give brief definitions of them because they are often used in a variety of ways, and the reader should understand the particular sense in which I am using them.

I begin with a chapter contrasting supportive and insight-oriented psychotherapy. The evaluation of patients for therapy is treated at length because it is the cornerstone of effective treatment. Goals of treatment, the qualifications of the therapist, and his behavior in the treatment hour are then discussed in successive chapters. After describing the strategy and tactics of supportive psychotherapy, the questions of transference, countertransference, and resistance in this mode of treatment are outlined.

The next five chapters deal with typical situations occurring during supportive psychotherapy and the tactical techniques that may be used to deal with them; the use of the dream in supportive psychotherapy is included in this section. The possibilities and means of changing from supportive to insight-oriented psychotherapy, and the reverse, are then discussed. A chapter describes the use of other therapeutic measures the therapist can consider, outside of the therapy hour. Termination of treatment and the problems related to it are the subjects of the book's concluding chapter.

Although I situate the practice of supportive psychotherapy against a background of psychoanalytic concepts, I have tried to stress issues that are paramount in the clinical setting. To practice psychotherapy without a set of guiding principles often leads to an aimless, improvisatory, and ultimately sterile technique. Certainly, spontaneity and improvisation can be valuable, but they are so only when they derive from experience and understanding. In a like manner, theory in and of itself has little value except as it informs and, in turn, is influenced by practice. Theory, when used uncritically, can suffocate the treatment process; used appropriately, it can be a beacon in an otherwise shadowy realm. The reader of this book will most benefit from it if he is actually engaged in doing supportive psychotherapy, and especially if he also has the opportunity to discuss his work with an experienced supervisor and other therapists.

While there are many references to insight-oriented psychotherapy throughout the book, I have not attempted to treat it systematically. This has been done by many other authors. Instead, I have limited myself to using the model of insight-oriented therapy only as a means of more clearly characterizing supportive work. As a result, the two modalities may seem to be completely dichotomous—which is quite untrue. Nevertheless, I believe it is helpful initially to distinguish these forms of treatment "in pure culture," one from the other. The reader who is practicing psychotherapy will, from his daily clinical experience, realize that the distinctions I have drawn here are only relative. If he has grasped the fundamental conceptual differences between supportive and insight-oriented psychotherapy, he will be aware of what he is doing at any given time and have a valid reason for doing it. This is simply another way of saying that life—the clinical situation—is far richer and more complex than any theoretical exposition. Although this can be frustrating for the therapist, it is what makes the practice of psychotherapy challenging and rewarding.

Contents

The Practice
of
Supportive
Psychotherapy

Supportive Psychotherapy and Insight-Oriented Psychotherapy

The distinctions between insight-oriented psychotherapy and supportive psychotherapy, as well as their very names, have been challenged by some authors. Nevertheless, I believe that there are substantial theoretical and practical differences between the two forms of treatment, and that psychotherapists should understand these differences in order to avoid any confusion over the goals and technical procedures which might weaken either therapeutic process. The names attached here to these modalities are neither very accurate nor sharply descriptive, but they are the terms that are most popularly used, and will continue to be used since the fate of neologisms is only too well known.

Although in the following pages these two forms of treatment are compared as if they were not only different from each other but virtually dichotomous in their aims and techniques, in reality they rarely exist in pure forms. Typically, over a period of time, most patients in supportive psychotherapy gain some insight into their behavior; similarly, it is difficult to conceive of a course of insight-oriented psychotherapy in which some supportive measures are not utilized.

Because no pronoun for male and female exists in English, I have used "he" throughout this book instead of the more awkward "he/she."

Additionally, while supportive psychotherapy is continually contrasted with insight-oriented psychotherapy, the therapist performing an evaluation for treatment should keep in mind that psychoanalysis may be the treatment of choice for carefully selected patients. In my view, psychoanalysis is chiefly distinguished from insight-oriented psychotherapy in that its goals are broader than symptom cure or relief, and include the further development of the patient as a person. This is important for every individual, but it is especially so for those patients whose maturity and richness of personality can have a powerful ameliorative effect on those with whom they work. Included among such individuals are not only all mental health professionals, but nonpsychiatric physicians and nurses, teachers, day-care center personnel, and clergy—to name but some of the groups to be considered. If the therapist doing an evaluation believes his patient may be an appropriate candidate for psychoanalysis, he should refer the patient to an analyst or a psychoanalytic clinic for further evaluation.

Despite the frequent use of the terms "insight-oriented psychotherapy" and "supportive psychotherapy," daily observations in the clinical setting confirm that there are profound differences of opinion and general unclarity regarding the theoretical nature of these treatment modalities. Even more striking, is that the technical differences between them are unclear, particularly those that relate to the practice of supportive psychotherapy. Repeatedly, one sees a stereotypical adherence to rules and procedures which, at best, may be appropriate to psychoanalysis or to insight-oriented psychotherapy. Such misuse of "psychoanalytic technique" has frequently led some therapists to reject anything that appears to be related to psychoanalysis.

The central difference between supportive and insight-oriented psychotherapy derives from the therapist's assessment of the patient. Supportive psychotherapy presumes a patient whose basic psychological "equipment" is more or less severely underdeveloped. There is little or no question of returning this individual to a former, healthy level of functioning. Optimally, this patient's mental capacities may be strengthened; more frequently, however, he may require help from external sources for an indefinite period of time.

The analogy to a patient with diabetes mellitus is useful here: The physician who treats the diabetic patient does not attempt, by some quixotic means, to cure the insulin deficiency; rather, he tries to minimize the worst effects of the illness by supplying insulin from outside the patient's body, he recommends a specific diet, he may prescribe insulin in order to substitute for the patient's deficiency in this hormone, and he may recommend other useful measures. Such therapeutic steps are, by their nature, quite different from those employed by a physician in treating, for example, pneumonia, for which a specific antibiotic is administered in order that an infectious process be eliminated and the patient's pulmonary tissues can revert to relative normalcy.

In fact, much of the physician's work is actually supportive and substitutive, and he would never regard such life-saving and life-enhancing measures as less worthy of his efforts and skill than the strictly curative therapies. It is not always so with psychotherapists who often seem to avoid, if not disdain, supportive psychotherapy—a modality of treatment which is indicated for a vast number of individuals, can also be literally life-saving, and that optimally can render the lives of many people more pleasurable and productive.

Supportive psychotherapy refers primarily, but not exclusively, to a form of treatment whose principal concern and focus is to strengthen mental functions that are acutely or chronically inadequate to cope with the demands of the external world and of the patient's inner psychological world. The acute deficiency, which we call a crisis, occurs when a patient whose life may previously have been in a state of reasonable equilibrium has more or less suddenly become deeply disturbed by a stressful event that may be real, symbolic, or fantasied, and that has precipitated a condition of "psychologic insufficiency."

A model for the work of supportive psychotherapy can be illustrated by a typical example of such a crisis. Carl B., a bright, athletic, college student, who functioned well throughout his life, was overwhelmed when his girlfriend jilted him. He was afflicted with pain, sadness, and anger, and his pride was hurt. The suffering was greater than any he had ever experienced in the past, and he found himself unable to tolerate it now. He found himself unable to study or even sit in a classroom. Even his formerly careful dress and personal hygiene deteriorated. He was unable to get enough sleep, his appetite was erratic, and he considered leaving school because he was unable to concentrate on the required work. He felt that he would never find anyone else to love; he felt empty and worthless without his girlfriend.

Carl believed that his intense sadness would continue indefinitely, and he was unable to think clearly about his situation or do anything about it. He felt so worthless that not only did he believe he was incapable of benefiting from help, but he felt that no one would even want to help him. He had fleeting thoughts of wishing he were dead but no specific thoughts about suicide. Such self-destructive fantasies seemed to reflect a turning of his anger from his girlfriend against himself; indeed, he began to experience himself as unlovable, hateful, and inept. The world itself seemed to reflect his feelings of emptiness, and so he withdrew from it into feelings of despair. His distorted view of the situation and his lack of "distance" from it did not allow him to appreciate that his pain would ever abate; he could not even imagine that there might be another woman in the world who could replace his girlfriend in his affections because the entire world had grown empty without her.

In such a situation, the therapist was able to perform a number of useful tasks since his evaluation of what had happened to the patient was reasonably correct. For example, he was able to identify some difficulties Carl had with reality testing, especially as to how he saw his future and how he viewed himself as a person. He had suffered a blow to his self-esteem and temporarily regarded himself as helpless, hopeless, and therefore worthless. He was also suffering psychological pain which he was unable to throw off by suppressing it (consciously putting it out of his mind) or by sublimating it in some effective way (that is, channeling it into some useful activity).

The initial interview in itself implicitly suggested to Carl that something could be done to alleviate his pain, and that at least the therapist did not find him as loathesome as he felt himself to be; in fact, he saw that the therapist was actually able to accept him as a fellow human being who was suffering and in need of help. The therapist attempted, verbally and nonverbally, to communicate to the patient that he appreciated the extent and the nature of his pain. Seeing his feelings understood by another person was very helpful to Carl because those feelings seemed less bizarre when they were identified and accepted by someone else, especially by someone whom he could respect. He began to feel less alone.

With the early establishment of some rapport, the psychotherapist attempted to do for the patient what the patient himself might have been able to do for a friend only a few weeks earlier: He carefully explored the realities of the situation; he helped the patient find realistic solutions; and when the patient had difficulty doing so, the therapist himself made some suggestions. He tactfully challenged Carl's unrealistic notions and illusions, and examined with him the possible consequences of one path of action or another. In this way, he helped the patient find alternatives; he made suggestions; he nurtured, guided, and helped him distinguish reality from fantasy. In short, he acted as an accepting, benevolent, level-headed parent who was "lending ego" to the patient at a time when the patient's own ego functions were momentarily inadequate to the needs of the situation.

In many crises, the impact of the crisis situation begins to lessen in a matter of days or weeks, and the patient's own ego resources resume adequate functioning. In fact, most psychological crises are actually surmounted without formal psychotherapy; mourning reactions are typical of these situations. Perhaps those individuals who are unable to deal with the usual life crises by themselves, or with the help of the people in their environment, are demonstrating some degree of "ego weakness." But I believe that a significant vulnerability need not be present for an individual to be overwhelmed by a stressful event. One's age, the particular qualities of the situation at that time, previous experience with such stress, the profound meaning of the stress to a given person—these and many other factors may be responsible for an individual's inability to cope with a particular event. It is also true that, despite everything, there are limits to the degree of suffering each human being can endure.

I suggest that the patients who are treated in supportive psychotherapy are fundamentally similar to Carl, the student in a crisis, except that their inadequate coping is usually chronic and may be expected to continue for an extended period of time. Furthermore, their problems are not necessarily precipitated by external events, even though such events may exacerbate their preexisting difficulties. For the most part, these patients readily succumb to stresses because they have specific insufficiencies or deficits in their ego which may be qualitative or quantitative.

In contrast to crisis intervention, the following pages will focus on relatively long-term, supportive psychotherapy which has been conceptualized for the most part, as a *substitutive* form of treatment, one that supplies the patient with those psychological elements that he either lacks entirely or possesses insufficiently. In effect, to an important extent this description of the nature of supportive psychotherapy implies that the therapist has grasped which psychological functions in his patient are deficient and, perhaps, can be strengthened or supplied. Such reinforcement usually concerns strengthening specific aspects of ego functioning although, as will be described later, there are other ways that support can be given.

A word of caution should be added in regard to the conceptualization of the "inadequate ego functions" described here. These insufficiencies should not be regarded as meaningless or random forms of psychic "scarring" or lacunae. They generally arise (mal)adaptively at some time in the patient's life, usually during his formative years; they may have appeared *de novo* later on or, more typically, they were reinforced by subsequent life events. In a subtle but powerful way, a person's attitudes, or pieces of his behavior, have an impact on the people in his environment who usually react to the behavior in such a way as to reinforce it, for better or worse.

The paranoid patient, for example, may develop enemies because of his suspiciousness; the masochist tends to bring out sadistic impulses in others; and compassionate, generous people usually evoke these qualities in those with whom they associate.

Furthermore, these insufficiencies, deficits, and rigid maladaptive patterns of mental functioning are not only the by-products of early developmental occurrences and later reflexive situations, but they are enmeshed in current dynamic situations and encompass, often in obscure ways, many of the elements of those situations. The suspicious individual, for example, who regularly is jealous of his wife every time she speaks to another man, may be projecting his own desire to have an extramarital affair. The fact that he deals with his "ego-alien" (unacceptable to his self) desires by projection is itself a compromise that is the result of numerous intense early and later experiences. The fact that the desire itself is abhorrent also constitutes a dynamic configuration. The more the therapist regards human behavior as complex amalgams of experience, impulse, defense, and adaptation, the better is he able to be helpful to his patient.

Although the fundamental work of supportive psychotherapy consists in shoring up ego functions, that is not the only role that this treatment modality can play. At times, and for certain patients more or less frequently, supportive psychotherapy provides them with the opportunity to air their feelings; it may offer them a symbolic form of love through the contact with an empathic, help-ing therapist; and it can help soothe angry, frightened, guilty, despairing or humiliated feelings, when the individual is unable to do so himself. Children need comforting when they are hurt; with maturity one never loses that need for comforting, but one becomes less dependent on others for it, and more able to soothe oneself. Some people, especially patients seen in supportive psychotherapy, have never learned to comfort themselves ade-quately at moments of distress, and so need to receive this help from others.

It is commonly said that, to a greater or lesser extent, supportive psychotherapy concerns the giving of "reassurance." This ill-de-fined notion has been used in various ways. Even worse, some individuals are not consistent in their use of this word. Reassur-ance generally means one of three different things. The first sug-gests that the therapist attempts to make the patient feel less pain by minimizing or denying unpleasant realities and by offering pleasing untruths. Unfortunately, this brings the therapist into collusion with the patient's misperceptions of reality; instead of working to enhance his reality testing, it undermines it.

In specific circumstances it may indeed be useful to reinforce a patient's denial of a frightening reality, such as impending death, when a justifiable element of hope, small as it may be, can be introduced. For example, a woman with metastatic breast can-cer had had several successful remissions following treatment with radiation therapy. She asked the psychiatrist, who had been called to see her because of depressive moods, whether he thought her condition was hopeless. He replied by saying that although her illness was serious and advanced, some patients with such illness have had their lives prolonged by several years. Such an attempt to foster hope in a patient is consistent with the medical facts.

A second meaning of reassurance relates to the therapist's empathic attitude which, of course, should be present in every form of treatment. The patient realizes that the therapist appreciates how he is feeling and that he even seems to be participating, to some extent, in the patient's suffering. When a patient experiences this resonance, it tends to undercut some of his feelings of isolation and makes him feel that the therapist understands him and is attentive to his needs. It also helps the patient to cooperate in his treatment.

Finally, the reassurance which I believe is most characteristic of supportive psychotherapy occurs when the patient is unable to exercise a realistic appraisal of a given situation because his cognitive functions, chiefly his reality testing, are operating inadequately. This may be because of long-standing ego deficits or because his ability to test reality is currently overwhelmed by massive feelings. In such situations the therapist works with the patient to help him become aware of genuine possibilities, of an alternative path, of possible contingencies, and assists him to make realistic and valid choices. Such tactics, common in counseling, are important in supportive psychotherapy.

It would be amiss to say that these techniques are never used in insight-oriented psychotherapy; however, in supportive psychotherapy they are more central to the strategy than they are in insight-oriented psychotherapy. The patient in supportive treatment who is frightened, confused, and generally unable to cope with his life, or cannot do so in some specific area, can find his anxiety diminished if he works with a therapist who, with respect, permits him to express his suffering and attempts to help him deal with those problems that he is truly unable to overcome by himself. Here again, the "substitutive" nature of supportive psychotherapy is evident, in contrast to the main strategy in insight-oriented psychotherapy, which is to provide the patient with insight into himself.

In contrast to the kind of supportive psychotherapy described, insight-oriented treatment is indicated for the individual whose enduring patterns of mental functioning—his "psychic structures"—are assumed to be reasonably well developed, and whose life history demonstrates that he has generally behaved adaptively and with pleasure. To an important extent, the task of such therapy is rehabilitative in that it helps the patient return to the former level of function which he enjoyed before one or more traumatic life events rendered his psychological functioning more or less dysfunctional. In a more far-reaching sense, such therapy may also assist the patient to develop more fully as a person—a development which had slowed down or ceased at some earlier time. The fundamental technical strategy here is centered on making conscious the forces within the patient that have led to his loss of psychological equilibrium. Thus, the goal is to enhance the patient's understanding of himself.

Insight-oriented psychotherapy seeks to alleviate painful emotional states—especially of anxiety and depression—modify ego-alien behaviors, moderate or perhaps even eliminate destructive activities, reduce neurotic symptoms, diminish behavior that leads to guilty feelings, and enhance relationships that have previously been ungratifying and even painful.

In recent years, psychotherapists have also become more sensitive to problems relating to the patient's self-concept, issues sometimes considered under the title of self-psychology. Most commonly these patients suffer from low self-esteem, feelings of humiliation, isolation, emptiness, embarrassment, and shame; less often they are intensely centered on their own worth and are grandiose. Their complaints, however, are not usually about these personality traits.

Insight-oriented psychotherapy attempts to work with the patient toward an increased awareness of the psychodynamic and, to some degree, psychogenetic framework within which the undesired psychological disturbances function. (The term psychodynamic refers to the interplay of conscious and unconscious, opposing mental forces in an individual, and the resultant symptoms that express that intrapsychic conflict. Typically, this conflict concerns sexual and aggressive impulses and the prohibitions against them. Psychogenetics refers to the psychological origins of these conflicts.) The anachronistic and self-destructive nature of such disturbances is clarified through a systematic reduction of the strength of those mental processes that keep significant feelings and thoughts from awareness. Through interpretations that the therapist makes of transference phenomena, fantasies, dreams, symptomatic acts, parapraxes (slips of the tongue, etc.), and patterns of behavior, the patient progressively becomes aware of his unconscious tendency to deal with current life situations in ways that are predominantly influenced by earlier, now outdated and maladaptive modes of dealing with stress and suffering.

The present, then, is illuminated cognitively and emotionally in terms of persistent behavior patterns and past experiences. The most poorly adaptive defense mechanisms, such as denial and projection, are modulated, and healthier ones, such as repression and sublimation, are fostered. Inhibitions that stand in the way of adult gratifications are explored so that the patient may be better able to satisfy his wishes. In the same way, neurotic symptoms, arising from intrapsychic conflicts, are explored with the expectation that the patient can eventually integrate these insights into his mental life and into his daily life so that both his inner world and his relationship to the external world can be brought into some reasonable harmony.

It is my impression that although insight-oriented psychotherapy is clearly an effective form of treatment for an appropriate patient, treated by a knowledgeable psychotherapist, the reason for its failure in many cases stems from its use with a patient for whom it is not appropriate. Such failures and stalemates not only waste the time of the patient and the psychotherapist and cost the patient an unnecessary expenditure of money, but frequently disenchant the therapist, especially the novice, with the efficacy of psychotherapy. He loses confidence both in himself as a therapist and in the value of psychological treatment. Worse still, he may angrily attribute such a failure to a lack of cooperativeness by the patient, because his own narcissistic mortification has obscured his role in the treatment difficulties. At other times, and for a variety of reasons, the patient and therapist may continue their meetings for an inordinately long time under the illusion that ongoing insight-oriented psychotherapy is actually taking place, when in fact patient and therapist are merely playing out a charade.

Although some of these difficulties in the therapy may arise from the patient's unrealistic goals, these may be shared, or even originate, with the psychotherapist who may entertain the fantasy that he is truly able to bring about substantial modifications in the patient's relatively enduring patterns of behavior, stereotypical affective responses, rigid defense patterns, distorted mental representations of self and object, symptom formations, maladaptive superego functions, and abrasive interpersonal relationships. It should be stressed that such patterns may be so encrusted and of such long standing that they can only be minimally modified, if at all. Instead of an endless, vain pursuit of a basic psychological change, which would entail profound alterations in psychological structures, the psychotherapist might be much more successful if he recognized that the patient needed specific kinds of help from external sources to compensate for his psychological deficiencies. That is the role of supportive psychotherapy.

Described schematically, insight-oriented psychotherapy is based on the assumption that the patient possesses psychological equipment of adequate quality, but that the function of this mental apparatus has to be freed up from those influences and conflicts that inhibit its fullest utilization. *In contrast, supportive psychotherapy assumes that the patient's psychological equipment is fundamentally inadequate.*

I have deliberately made a sharp contrast between the two forms of therapy and the individuals for whom they are indicated in order to clearly establish the issues at stake. In fact, although frequently these dichotomous characterizations will be referred to, the nuances and shadings that are always present will also be emphasized. Both forms of treatment usually overlap to a greater or lesser extent, and while at any given moment treatment may resemble one form more than the other, at a subsequent time the situation may be reversed. Thus the labels affixed to these modalities serve to refer to general directions and goals which are appropriate at a given stage of treatment; they are not fixed, pure forms of treatment that at all costs must always be kept apart.

2

Evaluating the Patient
for Therapy

The most knowledgeable and experienced psychotherapist will have only mediocre or poor results if he attempts to treat a patient in a modality of psychotherapy which is inappropriate for that patient. Consequently, the correct evaluation of the patient is perhaps the single most important procedure in the course of successful psychotherapy. This does not mean that the therapist cannot change his opinion about the patient's psychological status at any time during the treatment upon which he has embarked. In addition to correcting his initial evaluation, he may become aware that the patient himself has changed since an earlier assessment.

What is essential, however, is that throughout his work with the patient, the psychotherapist should be aware of the modality of treatment in which he is engaged, and of the patient's appropriateness for the kind of treatment he is receiving; this is a matter of correct "fit." Later I will describe how and under what circumstances the therapist may shift from a supportive to an insight-oriented form of psychotherapy, and vice versa, but at this point I will simply emphasize the importance of a correct evaluation as the basis for successful psychotherapy.

In carrying out an evaluation, one might be swayed in one direction or another by a particularly arresting trait in the patient's personality or behavior. The interviewer should defer his decision regarding the appropriate form of therapy until all the relevant aspects of the patient's life have been explored.

EGO DEFICIT

Since the typical patient for whom supportive psychotherapy is indicated demonstrates some significant degree of ego deficit or insufficiency, the assessment should be focused especially on those ego functions which are inadequate. By ego, I mean the collectivity of a series of psychological functions. Some of these are inborn and emerge and evolve in the course of normal growth and development. They include perception, locomotion, speech, memory, and the like. Others, predominantly psychological in character, include defenses (conscious and unconscious operations that maintain psychological equilibrium by keeping painful thoughts and feelings from overwhelming an individual), reality testing, self-observation or introspection, experience and appreciation of feelings, object relations, verbal ability, control of impulses—especially those derived from sexual and aggressive desires, judgment, cognition, the possession of sublimatory assets, and the tolerance of mental pain.

The therapist will also want to know how the patient has fared in the outside world: in school, at work, and in his relationships with other people. Has he married, and what sort of spouse is he? If a parent, how does he get along with his children? Has he previously received psychiatric treatment, and how successful was it? Does he abuse alcohol or drugs? What massive traumas has he suffered, especially in his early years? How has he reacted toward the important losses and the defeats of everyday life, as well as the successes that have come his way?

It must always be kept in mind that an apparent inadequacy of any ego function may either be the consequence of a disturbance in development or represent a regression subsequent to a significant life stress. Only a careful history can clarify this matter, and with a relatively uncommunicative patient, it may not be possible to do so until a later time. For example, a severely depressed patient may not be able to describe what precipitated his current depressed state. However, when the depression is less severe, he may be able to describe the events leading up to his illness.

As mentioned earlier, the therapist may be unduly impressed by one striking aspect of a patient's psychological makeup or social situation. For example, alcoholic patients are often regarded as appropriate candidates for supportive psychotherapy because of the addictive nature of their drinking. However, a complete assessment of a given individual might reveal that he possesses other qualities that could outweigh his addiction: for example, there may be evidence that he had richly benefited from previous psychotherapy, or his current drinking problem may have been provoked by a recent overwhelming stress, or had begun by the desire to deaden pain from organic illness. This patient may also demonstrate a good social history, an ability to be introspective, professional productivity, and creativity.

In a contrary sense, an interviewer might be overly influenced by the achievements of a patient who has been, for example, referred for therapy because of a peptic ulcer. This patient may be articulate and have had a higher education, but he is easily overwhelmed by even modest stresses, denies his role in many of the complicated life situations in which he frequently finds himself, and shows a marked inability to restrain his aggressive impulses. Such a patient, despite an aura of social success, may actually possess more ego deficiencies than the alcohol abuser described above, and supportive psychotherapy may be indicated for him. Thus the relative strength of all criteria being examined is of the utmost significance.

REALITY TESTING

The ability to test reality is perhaps the single most important and useful yardstick to determine if a patient is psychotic. Unfortunately, it can easily be misused because it is misunderstood. The ability to "test reality" is not to be understood as a lens which more or less correctly captures the actual qualities of the objects on which it is focused. In fact, deficiencies in reality testing are always selective and cluster along specific psychodynamic lines. Furthermore, it is hardly an "all or none" phenomenon, but one with many gradations. Finally, it is not a fixed function, but one that can fluctuate considerably. Poor reality testing suggests that such functions as perception, judgment, and evaluation, instead of being relatively free from conflict, so that they are generally in agreement with other people's perceptions, are flooded with conflict, making them less congruent with what is generally observed.

Betty R., for example, usually showed fair reality testing except when she thought of what other people thought of her, whereupon she became suspicious and angry, believing that they regarded her at best as promiscuous and at worst as a prostitute—a fantasy that arose from unconscious ideas she had about herself. The other side of the same coin is reflected in the common observation that even a floridly psychotic patient who is hallucinating and delusional will usually have maintained intact some portion of cognitive function. The therapist, doing supportive psychotherapy, can work with those reliable aspects of the patient's reality testing to achieve a greater congruence with reality. He will not necessarily deal with the defective reality testing as a symptom of conflict, but will attempt to help the patient perceive more accurately.

Again, one should determine if problems with reality testing are of lifelong duration (a "process" phenomenon) or are the consequences of a current regression.

IMPULSE DISORDERS

There are some individuals whose lives constitute a series of more or less disastrous behavioral events; treatment with them becomes a picaresque novel. They enter each hour breathless and relate the latest "catastrophe" that has overtaken them, rarely suggesting any awareness of their role in the disaster. In an evaluation, such a history suggests that the patient has a preference for action over talking and thinking, and has pronounced difficulties in delaying impulses. Rash and sometimes destructive behavior may represent either a "primary" impulse disorder or be the result of a recently precipitated emotional disturbance; the latter is, of course, much more amenable to being influenced than is the former, and such patients may benefit from insight-oriented psychotherapy. This is much less likely with patients with "primary impulse disorders." This condition is poorly understood.

On the one hand, it seems to be, at least to some extent, related to constitutional influences. On the other, there is some evidence that points to an inadequate development of the ability to delay gratification of impulses.

One must be careful not to regard an individual as "primarily" impulsive who is actually an active, "motoric" person. In the same way, mistakes can be made in deciding whether an individual is thoughtful or passive. The inhibition of action may be caused by an underlying depression, and excessive activity may suggest a manic state. These matters,once again, underline the necessity of a *total* evaluation of each patient, studying strengths as well as weaknesses.

If a patient presents with a lifelong history of poor impulse control, supportive psychotherapy is usually the treatment of choice. This patient can be shown, to some extent and over a period of time, how destructive his impulsive behavior can be to himself and to others. He can be shown that there are rewards in delaying his impulses, and that not only will he be rewarded by the people around him, but that he himself may be gratified by the change in his behavior. (However, the inability to experience such gratification itself suggests another area of serious developmental arrest.)

THE "ATTRACTIVE" PATIENT

It has been alleged that psychotherapists are only interested in treating the young, attractive, verbal, intelligent, and successful patient—the "YAVIS." Although there is some truth in this, as in any generalization, the criticism merely gives voice to the obvious fact that what is less disordered is more readily corrected—whether it is the body, the mind, a machine, or society. Nevertheless, more severe disturbances, while usually more difficult to treat, can be modified to a significant extent. The task appears more formidable for the therapist who lacks the ability or the experience of practicing supportive psychotherapy.

AGE

If one examines the YAVIS formula, it becomes a mere catchword. Youth, in and of itself, is a highly variable factor in the assessment for treatment; some patients in every age group may be appropriate candidates for supportive or insight-oriented psychotherapy. Attractiveness, aside from being subjective and vague, is irrelevant except insofar as it leads a therapist to make a wrong decision about the appropriate form of treatment for a given patient.

INTELLIGENCE

Intelligence is a factor which under certain circumstances may prove to be of significance. Unfortunately, there is little data concerning the influence of intelligence on the course of any form of psychotherapy. Since psychological development is dependent, in large part, on the presence of normal brain function, it is clear that infants who are cerebrally dysfunctional frequently grow up with some psychological impairment. Such individuals may present with cognitive difficulties, primary impulse disorders, a poor school and work performance, and the like. For such patients, supportive psychotherapy as a substitutive process, in which there is a considerable "lending" of ego, is strongly indicated.

On the other hand, some therapists have presumed that, because a patient is highly intelligent, he is necessarily a candidate for insight-oriented psychotherapy. In fact, intelligence may be used as a powerful shield, or resistance, behind which an intellectual patient can hide.

An illustration of this is provided by Roberta W., a graduate student in philosophy, who came for treatment because of the last of a series of disastrous love affairs. She had, she announced, "read all of Freud" and was damned if she was "going to listen to any of that crap about penis envy." From the outset, therapy increasingly took on the appearance of a debate, with the patient constantly challenging the therapist's cultural and intellectual background. Feeling devalued, he valiantly but unsuccessfully tried to maintain his self-esteem. As a result, he overlooked the patient's underlying depression. By the time he did grasp the fact that Miss W. was in despair it was too late and she abruptly ended the treatment. This patient might have benefited from a period of supportive work, perhaps with antidepressant medication. When her depression subsided, a reevaluation could have been undertaken to ascertain what the next phase of therapy should be.

VERBAL ABILITY

I have never found that verbal ability, in and of itself, is a useful criterion in evaluating a patient. All psychotherapy, almost by definition, is a verbal form of treatment, and necessarily the patient must be able to express himself with some modicum of clarity. But beyond that, verbal ability is not a critical factor in the assessment. Indeed, as with intelligence, an intellectualized, polysyllabic speech might lead a therapist to assume that a patient is a candidate for insight-oriented psychotherapy when instead supportive work is indicated.

There are some taciturn individuals who do not talk either during or outside of a psychotherapy hour. This does not necessarily represent a characterological disturbance but may simply indicate that these people are not especially verbal, and they go comfortably through life saying very little even to close friends and family. Such patients, even if they are suffering, may have little to say about their pain; their remarks are barely spontaneous, if at all, and the evaluation often threatens to break down into a series of questions posed by the therapist and some brief responses by the patient. This trait may suggest that supportive treatment rather than insight work is indicated. If other criteria support this decision, supportive psychotherapy should be recommended, with the thought that the patient's parsimonious speech may be a reactive phenomenon, and that, in fact, the patient might more appropriately be doing insight work.

Some patients may generally be reasonably verbal but they are not so during the evaluation when their silence may represent anxiety, depression or resistance to treatment.

SILENCE

Silence may also represent a profound lack of basic trust, an immediate negative transference reaction, or some unidentified reality factor. For example, Mrs. Bertha V., a middle-aged survivor of the holocaust, thought her therapist had an uncanny resemblance to a guard in the concentration camp where she had been confined, and who had caused her to suffer extraordinary physical and emotional pain. She was unable to tell this to her therapist because it seemed too childish and irrational. In another situation, Paul M., a young, rebellious student who had been locked in an intense struggle with his father, immediately and consciously equated his middle-aged male therapist with his rigid controlling father and stubbornly refused to be interviewed. Fortunately, he was able to announce his inability to work with the interviewer and transfer to a younger therapist was made.

In still another situation, a therapist who was an incessant smoker intensely disturbed a patient who was too embarrassed to confront him with his thoughts and feelings about smoking and lapsed into silence.

Initial and continuing silence may be dealt with through questions, confrontations, clarifications, and perhaps a superficial interpretation. However, if the silence does not diminish, it would be wise to begin psychotherapy in a supportive manner until the therapist develops a better understanding of the patient.

SUCCESS IN SCHOOL OR WORK

The success of a patient in school and at work is another important but relative factor. Good performance does not clearly indicate that a patient should be in insight-oriented psychotherapy. However, a lifelong history of failure at least suggests the possibility of a developmental arrest. But here again, work, like love, is one of the principal areas of human behavior that is subject to conflict. This is particularly notable when a formerly successful individual begins to experience difficulties in working, following on the heels of a specific stress; this was illustrated in Chapter I, in the vignette of Carl B., the college student whose girlfriend left him. Poor school performance in children is another common example of the intrusion of conflict in work.

SOCIAL AND CULTURAL FACTORS

Social and cultural circumstances must be carefully considered here. An individual from a poverty-level family may not only have not been successful in school and work, but may have grown up feeling quite hopeless—not altogether incorrectly—about the possibilities for achievement. This would be in marked contrast to the patient who was raised in a middle-class family, where he was encouraged to achieve and was given many opportunities and rewards. I shall not deal here with the issue of ethnic, social, sexual, cultural, and religious differences between therapist and patient. Nevertheless, it is a most important matter, and lack of insight into the problems of stereotypes and biases can create significant difficulties in treatment unless it is carefully kept in view and understood.

From the foregoing, it is apparent that the YAVIS formula turns out to be, generously speaking, a witticism rather than a valid description of the evaluation process; it is inaccurate both for patients for whom insight-oriented psychotherapy is recommended and those for whom supportive work is indicated.

INTROSPECTION

The inability to be introspective (or psychologically minded) is perhaps the most frequent basis on which the decision to recommend supportive psychotherapy is made. The individual who lacks this trait is more or less unable to "step outside of himself" and view his behavior dispassionately and with some degree of objectivity. For example, Mr. William T. came to a clinic complaining of "depression," stating that his troubles all stemmed from his wife's nagging. This may have been accurate, but he did not recognize how he contributed to her behavior, nor did he admit to himself that he felt totally helpless in dealing with her. In supportive treatment he slowly was able to see that he had some responsibility for his marital difficulties; the therapist also helped him explore different ways in which he could cope more effectively with his wife.

The nonintrospective patient, like Mr. T., tends to implicate people in his environment for his troubles. He usually also shows a marked lack of curiosity about his behavior, his feelings, his fantasies, and his dreams.

Instead of blaming identifiable people or specific events as the source of their difficulties, some patients believe that unknowable, occult forces are working against them: fate, their astrological sign, a hex that was placed on them, possession by malevolent spirits, or a punishment decreed by a vengeful god. Although such patients may not be able to relinquish these beliefs, in supportive psychotherapy they may achieve a greater tolerance of their condition than they had previously had.

A special aspect of deficient introspection concerns an individual's difficulty in both knowing what he is feeling at any given moment, and being unable to express his feelings. This condition has been called, somewhat vaguely, alexithymia, and is also a relative indication for supportive psychotherapy. In evaluating a patient, the therapist should be careful not to confuse this condition with the imprecise terms used by some people to describe their feelings. Words such as "upset," "spacey" and "paranoid" are usually popular catchwords that actually reflect specific feelings that can often be identified by further questioning.

SUBLIMATORY CHANNELS

The presence of "sublimatory channels," that is, socially useful activities, is of considerable value in helping human beings discharge sexual and, especially, aggressive tensions. An aggressive, rebellious teenager who can regularly play a vigorous game of basketball will often find that much of his pent-up steam has blown off. If, in the course of evaluation, a patient is unable to report any pleasurable leisure time activities, he should be questioned further as to the kind of life he leads. Sometimes his work has expanded to fill almost all his waking hours. His family may find this objectionable, but if the patient is comfortable with such a monolithic existence, there may be little to be gained and much to be lost in trying to make him experience his compulsion to work as an undesirable activity. Certainly, if his zeal in working is having a bad effect on his family, he must be confronted with this fact. Otherwise, such compulsive behavior serves defensive purposes, and if it is not objectionable to the patient it should not be disturbed.

Sublimatory channels not only are escape valves for unexpressed drive impulses, but can foster a better self-regard and elevate a patient's depressive mood. For reasons that are not well

understood, these activities sometimes can be helpful for psychotic or severely regressed patients; perhaps this is related to a
mobilization and integration of "body ego" (a profound sense of
one's physical self) which is the bedrock on which mental ego
rests.

TOLERANCE OF SUFFERING

Even a casual observation of some psychologically disturbed
individuals quickly establishes whether they can tolerate more
than trivial amounts of mental suffering. Usually, the tolerance
relates to anxiety and depression, but it can also refer to any
painful feelings: guilt, shame, jealousy, envy, humiliation, and
the like. The patient who loudly insists that his psychic pain is
intolerable, that he must immediately be given medication to quell
his suffering, and who may actually display tantrums, should best
be referred for supportive psychotherapy where there is little likelihood that the traumatic episodes of his past will be reexperi-
enced in the present, along with the frustrations occasioned by
the treatment itself.

In this respect, the most powerful resurgence of one's past
typically occurs in the development of transference. This is discussed in more detail in Chapter VII, but here I am concerned
with the patient's possible tolerance of this reaction. When transference can be experienced and tolerated by a patient, it becomes
the pivot of insight-oriented psychotherapy, where it is fostered,
interpreted, and worked through. Transference is a complex phenomenon, but seems to depend on an individual's object relations—that is, his ability to maintain conscious and unconscious
mental representations of others in whom he has an enduring
emotional investment. Such an ability usually permits an individual to continue to maintain that emotional investment in another
person despite disappointments, and even the death of the other
person.

RELATIONSHIPS WITH OTHERS

Smooth interpersonal relationships do not adequately provide
good information about the quality of a patient's object relations.

Some narcissistic individuals, psychopaths, or simply those who are socially adept may be able to "get along" extraordinarily well with others, but their actual emotional involvement with them may be slight or nonexistent. A therapist evaluating a patient will ask about the patient's relationships with and feelings toward the people close to him—parents, spouse, siblings, and children. He will inquire about friendships and how long they have endured. Sometimes a person's object relations may be revealed by a loving attitude to a present or former pet. One should not assume that an individual who leads a relatively solitary existence necessarily has poor object relations. Such isolation may reflect a fear of intimacy, shyness, or a profound disappointment with a former object. It is enough, at this point, simply to note that patients who have poor object relations should be considered for supportive psychotherapy because that form of treatment does not depend on the development of transference.

EGO DEFENSES

Throughout these pages will be repeated discussions of ego defenses. In the evaluation, one must assess the kinds and relative importance of a patient's defenses. A patient who relies heavily on only one or two defenses is less apt to modify them than one who has a larger repertoire of ways to protect himself from painful thoughts or feelings. Furthermore, although all defenses in effect say "no" to some inner or outer piece of reality, projection, denial, and splitting are especially maladaptive because they completely oppose the development of a self-observing attitude during therapy. If these defenses are prominent and not readily modifiable, it speaks in favor of assigning that patient to supportive therapy.

TRUST

It goes without saying that although the presence of a certain amount of basic trust is necessary in every kind of therapeutic relationship, a significant weakness in trust (put differently, a high degree of suspiciousness or even paranoiac attitudes) is a strong indication for supportive psychotherapy. Of course, in supportive psychotherapy, too, the absence of basic trust may create profound difficulties with which the therapist must deal in order to maintain a therapeutic relationship. The technical aspects of this will be discussed in a later chapter.

SOMATIC PROBLEMS

Patients who are referred for the psychotherapeutic treatment of functional somatic symptoms such as obesity or one of the classic psychosomatic disorders do not, I believe, benefit much from insight-oriented psychotherapy unless they are also concerned about concomitant psychological problems. If the patient wishes help with the emotional problems that are bothering him and which are his primary focus, he may be an appropriate candidate for insight-oriented psychotherapy, and one can hope that the somatic matters may be modified along with improvement of the emotional difficulties. However, patients who are prone to "somatize" and deny the presence of emotional problems, as well as hypochondriacal patients, are often referred by their medical doctors to a psychotherapist. For many, if not most of these patients, supportive psychotherapy is usually indicated if this decision continues to be borne out by other factors observed during the evaluation.

Mrs. Emily F., an obese, sad, middle-aged woman who had had an episode of depression following the breakup of her marriage began to see a therapist in what was supposed to be insight-oriented therapy. However, she spent every hour discussing the difficulty, indeed the "impossibility," of losing weight. She grew highly critical of her therapist for not being able to "get her" to diet successfully. The therapist finally suggested that Mrs. F. see someone specifically for help in weight reduction while continuing to see him in order to work on her emotional problems. The second therapist was able to work with the patient on the issue of her diet by using techniques aimed at modifying her eating behavior. Psychotherapy then progressively became more directed toward the patient's insight into her dependency and competitiveness.

With another obese patient the same strategy failed and the patient continued to use his insight-oriented psychotherapy session to ruminate on his "weight problem." The therapist sought a consultation where the patient declared that his only problem was his weight and that it was "just a bad habit." This man was found to be poorly introspective; he had a lifelong history of poor performance at school and later at the jobs he had held; he was markedly dependent and flatly told the consultant that he just wanted to lose weight. The consultant also noted extensive use of denial and not infrequent splitting. Supportive psychotherapy was recommended and the original therapist shifted to that mode of treatment in which he became more directive in helping the patient. Both of these patients had had only the most cursory evaluations, and the issues discussed here were not specifically identified.

REFERRALS AND MOTIVATION

Some patients are referred to the therapist by their medical doctor, family member, teacher or employer. Such a patient may come grudgingly, and even be suspicious of the therapist. If the therapist has ascertained that there is a firm indication for supportive psychotherapy, he can do no less than strongly encourage the patient to enter treatment. He should explain why therapy is indicated, what the patient can expect it to do for him, and how it is conducted. If the patient refuses—and is not homicidal or suicidal (in which case he should be involuntarily committed to a hospital)—the therapist should urge him to carefully consider treatment and a return appointment should be arranged to provide the opportunity for a further discussion of the matter.

Some therapists despair of ever enlisting in therapy these poorly motivated patients. While it may indeed be difficult, the patient who is suffering will often agree to at least try therapy for a while. Mr. Arthur J., an elderly man, was heavily burdened by a sense of guilt arising from his conviction that he had caused his wife's sudden death from a myocardial infarction. He was brought to the therapist by his son and with considerable reluctance agreed to return the following week. Skeptically, he continued to return for further visits. The therapist was of benefit to him by first helping him recognize the unreality of his ideas, and second, by giving him "permission" to be less self-condemnatory and punitive. In this case, the therapist was assisted by the patient's children, who helped him build an alliance through which some useful therapeutic work was carried out.

"ENERGY"

One criterion that should be particularly considered in the evaluation of a patient, and which is rarely described, relates to the degree of physical and mental "energy" the patient possesses. It is difficult to adequately describe this factor which relates to life-long patterns of passivity or activity. Such a pattern may have important constitutional roots, but regardless of its origins, whether biological, learned, or some combination of both, it may be sufficiently powerful to prevent the patient from mobilizing himself to make the effort required to effect some changes in his life. He may feel more comfortable in foregoing many things rather than wanting them or being able to expend the energy to obtain them. Such a patient's physical behavior itself may reflect his passivity as manifested in movements, posture, and speech.

Betty R. was referred to a therapist by a colleague in another city. She was 23 years old and had, yet again, been hospitalized earlier that year for another ill-described "breakdown." She slowly entered the therapist's office, head bent forward and shoulders drooping. Her gait was tentative and she walked like a child wearing her mother's high-heeled shoes. When invited to sit down, she slumped into a chair. She made no spontaneous remarks and such answers as she did give were vague, fragmentary, and slow. Frequently, instead of giving a verbal response, she grimaced or shrugged her shoulders as if to say, "I don't know, and I don't care."

The therapist thought that her lethargy might be due to the medication she was receiving—a narcoleptic and an antidepressant. However, when the medications were slowly discontinued over the ensuing months, there was no demonstrable change in Miss R.'s passivity. She was seen over the next three years and, although at times she was slightly more animated, she never showed anything approximating the degree of energy appropriate for a person of her age. Subsequent talks with members of her family revealed that she had been like that since she was 11 years old. Supportive psychotherapy was somewhat successful in several ways: the patient had only one brief hospital stay during the three years; she held a full-time job, supporting herself and maintaining her own apartment; she stopped abusing hard drugs and alcohol; and her desperate promiscuity ceased. When treatment was terminated because the patient returned to her hometown, she regressed and began the first of a new series of hospitalizations.

THE ROLE OF DIAGNOSIS

A common error in assessment is utilizing a clinical diagnosis, such as is outlined in the Diagnostic and Statistic Manual, as the principal factor in deciding whether to assign a patient to supportive or insight-oriented psychotherapy. While in some respects it is both useful and necessary for the therapist to make such a diagnosis, I believe it is of limited value in deciding on the kind of psychotherapy that is indicated for a given patient. In and of itself, the clinical diagnosis is not the equivalent of a therapeutic or prognostic diagnosis.

The diagnosis of the borderline personality, for example, is frequently given to many patients referred for supportive psychotherapy, although it is generally agreed that there can be a considerable difference between the most and the least disturbed of these patients. The difference can be attributed to the variety and severity of the particular ego weakness or deficits present in an individual patient. As a result, it seems that the patients diagnosed as having a borderline personality comprise an extraordinarily heterogeneous group of people (witness the variety of descriptions) who have prominent ego deficiencies. This is in contrast to patients whose primary diagnosis is classified as a neurosis, who are distinguished by the prominence of specific debilitating symptoms resulting from psychological *conflicts*—phobias, conversion reactions, and the like—and whose egos are not significantly deficient. Nevertheless, despite having diagnosed one individual as borderline and another as neurotic, one cannot conclusively determine which form of therapy is appropriate for these individuals. That decision must be based on additional criteria.

Indeed, the same problem confronts the therapist in respect to patients in every diagnostic category, whether it be personality disorder, psychosis, affective illness, neurosis, or even organic brain syndrome. In all of these categories, one will always find at least some patients who are appropriate candidates for supportive treatment.

As much can be said for patients diagnosed as "borderline personalities" or for patients with character disorders, problems related to drug and alcohol abuse, and organic brain syndromes. Every experienced therapist has worked unsuccessfully with neurotic patients in insight-oriented psychotherapy, and the possibilities of treating some schizophrenic patients, when in remission, with insight therapy are well known. The criteria for one form of treatment or the other are more important than the diagnosis assigned to the patient. Obviously, mistakes regarding disposition will be made, but little or no harm is done if the errors are identified with promptness and appropriate changes are made.

EXTENDED EVALUATION

If the therapist finds that he is unable to make a reasonable assessment of a patient regarding disposition to insight-oriented or supportive psychotherapy, I find it useful to recommend that the patient meet with the therapist for a specified number of additional hours—as many as 10 or 12—during which time the matter of the type of treatment can be explored more carefully. One can explain to the patient that these meetings will serve to better identify his problems and how best to deal with them. At the same time, the therapist will have an extended opportunity to observe the manner in which the patient behaves during this period, which can be an additional aid in evaluation.

Such a procedure seems preferable to the so-called trial of treatment, since it commits neither the patient nor the therapist to a given course of action, and does not carry with it the disappointment the patient may experience if he is told that, after all, he is not an appropriate patient for the type of psychotherapy elected. In effect, however, the additional hours spent in this extended evaluation do constitute an onset of treatment and, as such, often give the therapist a fairly good idea of how treatment in the modality considered will proceed.

ACCEPTING EVALUATIONS BY OTHERS

A common problem in the evaluation of patients arises from the way the referral has been made and by whom. Many junior professionals —residents, or other trainees working in clinics and mental health centers—have patients referred to them by senior professionals who, for one reason or another, are eager for their younger colleague to begin treatment with the patient. Since the usual search, on the part of the trainee, is for a person who is designated as a "very good patient," that is, highly appropriate for insight-oriented psychotherapy, the referring professional often describes the patient in terms that may be somewhat or even grossly misleading. If the referring individual is someone in authority, the junior person may be less careful in evaluating the patient than he would be if the patient had come to him without the "authoritative" referral.

A therapist should rarely, if ever, accept the evaluation of a patient that was done by someone else, especially if it means that he commits himself to seeing the patient for an extended period of time. Even the patient's history should not necessarily be assumed to be accurate; it may be skewed in one direction or another and should be asked for once more. In short, the therapist who actually intends to work with the patient should review all the evaluatory criteria, establish his own clinical and therapeutic diagnosis, and make at least a tentative prognosis.

From the foregoing it can be seen that evaluating a patient for therapy, no less than carrying out supportive psychotherapy, is a procedure that requires knowledge and concern.

3

The Therapeutic Agreement

The therapeutic agreement between the patient and the therapist in supportive psychotherapy is in many ways similar to that arranged with patients seen in insight-oriented psychotherapy. Arrangements as to the time of meeting, the frequency of meetings, the handling of absences, the fee to be paid, and similiar matters, are generally alike in both forms of therapy.

However, the therapist should bear in mind that the patients in need of supportive psychotherapy are very often either in the midst of an intense emotional upheaval or have been chronically unable to cope with life's stresses. Consequently, greater latitude should be taken in the setting up of therapeutic agreements with these patients than might be indicated for those individuals who enjoy a greater measure of ego strength. For instance, latenesses and absences may be more frequent with patients in supportive psychotherapy, and although such behavior can and should be dealt with, a more flexible approach to these problems may be required than would be appropriate with patients in insight-oriented psychotherapy.

Nevertheless, the problem of adhering to the agreement should be discussed in an open, empathic, and nonpunitive manner, and the patient helped to overcome the difficulty, for example, in keeping his appointments regularly and on time. Not only do such discussions, when held in a compassionate spirit, tend to establish good rapport between the therapist and the patient, but they signal to the patient that the therapist is concerned and is committed to setting limits to the patient's behavior; in this way the therapist tacitly demonstrates a practical concern for the patient. At the same time, it is also a step towards assisting the patient to achieve greater control over his behavior, a change which would find wider applicability in his everyday life. Such a "corrective" approach contrasts with the clear emphasis, in insight-oriented psychotherapy, on trying to understand the meaning of the patient's behavior.

The therapist should be aware that patients in supportive psychotherapy may require additional kinds of help in the course of their contact with the therapist. For example, seeing the patient as an outpatient on a regular basis may, at some point, either prove to be inadequate for his needs or have to be temporarily abandoned. Such patients not infrequently need brief hospitalization, but occasionally they may require a longer inpatient stay. The use of psychotropic medication is frequently indicated, and changes in the particular medication prescribed or alterations in dosage may become necessary. Vocational rehabilitation for some of the more disabled patients is useful not only as a therapeutic adjunct and as a measure to enhance self-esteem, but most importantly, as a means of enabling the patient to earn a living.

There are a wide variety of group arrangements, ranging from group therapy to community support groups, which are especially useful if the group has a specific focus which meets the needs of a particular patient. Meetings with a patient's spouse or other family members are often useful and at times may be mandatory. Work with the more regressed patient, the suicidal patient, and the violent patient is considerably enhanced by enlisting the cooperation of family members. This can be done in a variety of ways ranging from conjoint sessions to separate counseling with these relatives.

At times, it may be necessary for the therapist to consider transferring the patient to another therapist; this may arise when the therapeutic situation is stalemated or when transference or countertransference reactions have become intense and unresolvable. The guiding principle is to exercise flexibility in all aspects of the therapeutic process.

The variability and flexibility of treatment of patients in supportive psychotherapy often imposes an additional stress on some therapists. There are some who cannot easily tolerate irregularity and the shifting of focus and style; it may be wiser for such therapists to avoid practicing supportive psychotherapy or to drastically limit themselves to doing perhaps only one hour of it each week. Even those psychotherapists who are able to work with difficult patients in supportive psychotherapy have found that there is a definite limit to how many hours a week they can spend with these patients, especially those who are markedly disturbed. However, the therapist who sees each patient in supportive psychotherapy once or twice a month for twenty minutes can work with up to eight or ten patients in a month by devoting but one hour a week to them collectively. In passing, I believe that the fees for the shorter hours should be scaled in proportion to the time spent, even if third party payers permit otherwise. This, however, is something that each therapist must decide for himself, because it is hardly useful to the patient if his therapist harbors resentment towards him because he pays less than standard fees.

I have found that many therapists seem to be able to carefully follow only one or two severely regressed patients at a time; this is assuming that they have a strong commitment to working with these patients despite the expenditure of time beyond the therapeutic hour itself. Needless to add, there are therapists whose tolerance for working with regressed patients is much greater. However, it is not unusual that one or two of these patients can cause a therapist more difficulty and a greater outlay of time and effort than might several patients seen in insight-oriented psychotherapy. Phone calls from the patient's family, from the patient himself, his teachers or employers, the police or other authorities, visits to the emergency room on weekends and nights—all this and more, may be part of the treatment picture when working with some patients in supportive psychotherapy. Suicidal impulses, ranging from gestures to serious attempts, and homicidal threats also may need to be dealt with, placing additional stress upon the therapist both emotionally and by cutting deeply into his time.

Most of the patients followed in supportive psychotherapy are seen in mental health centers, psychiatric clinics, and other public institutions. Many of them pay low fees and often no fee at all.

This may be a problem in itself because not infrequently the treatment and the therapist are devalued by the patient who feels that inexpensive or free treatment cannot be of much value. For that reason, it is desirable that the patient should pay a fee, no matter how small it is, commensurate with his financial situation. However, in some institutions, such as veterans hospitals, no fee is required from the patient. In these situations, the therapist should deal with the patient in precisely the same way as if he were paying a full fee for the service received.

In other situations, such as psychiatric clinics, where the patient does pay a fee, he realizes that the therapist, very often a resident or other trainee, does not receive the money which actually goes to the institution. When initiating treatment, the therapist should be alert to this question, and when the matter of fee is discussed he should explore it with the patient if he hears anything that suggests that the patient has some concern about it. This problem is no less important in making a therapeutic agreement with a patient in supportive psychotherapy than it is with one in insight-oriented treatment.

It has often been said that psychotherapy begins at the first contact between the patient and the therapist, even if that initial contact is by telephone; this view holds just as well in supportive psychotherapy as for any other form. There is, however, one significant difference: Since the patients usually seen in supportive psychotherapy tend to be more regressed or fixated than those in insight-oriented psychotherapy, it is therefore more difficult for them to develop a working, trusting relationship with their doctor. This places a particular responsibility on the therapist to work, from the outset, to establish a modicum of rapport between the patient and himself. By rapport, it is not meant that the patient should "like" the therapist, but that he should have a sense that the therapist is concerned about his well-being and regards him as a worthwhile person.

In the same way, it is not necessary for the therapist to "like" the patient. This issue can be distorted by patients and therapists alike, who often insist that the therapists must "like," "care for" and even "love" their patients. I would suggest that if a therapist has especially positive feelings for his patients he engage in some careful self-scrutiny to ascertain that these feelings do not represent a significant countertransference reaction. What the therapist should realistically feel towards his patients is a positive regard for them as human beings; he should be able to respond empathically to them; and he should be devoted to helping them, as best as his skill permits, within the framework of psychotherapy. If therapists could generally behave in this manner, they would be serving their patients far more usefully than by simply "liking" them.

Within the above framework, it is still inevitable that a therapist will not have the same feelings toward all his patients. Those with whom therapy works more effectively and who struggle to understand themselves and to integrate their insight into their daily lives will obviously evoke different feelings in the therapist than will those who constantly attack the therapist and devalue treatment. Similarly, one cannot escape the fact that the sharing of a common value system by patient and therapist also affects the therapist's concern.

The development of rapport will prove to be most arduous if the patient harbors significant hostile or other negative feelings towards the therapist. The therapist should be attuned to subtle evidences of negative feelings and deal with them as early as possible (the overt manifestations are too obvious to be missed). Failure to do so typically leads to the patient's leaving treatment prematurely and often precipitously. These negative attitudes can be dealt with in a direct, noncritical, nonretaliatory, nonargumentative way; the issue should be broached in a spirit of seeking to discover, with the patient, the source of his disruptive feelings towards therapy and the therapist.

In situations in which the patient is impelled to seek treatment because of his mental anguish, the prospect of dealing with his hostility is obviously much better than in those instances when he has been compelled to enter therapy against his will, because of a court order or pressure from a family member, third person or agency. However, not all manifestations of hostility necessarily indicate the absence of rapport. At times, the potential for rapport can be present even though the patient seems to be fiercely antagonistic to the therapist. Although one should try to understand what the anger or hatred represents in order to deal most effectively with it, such understanding may not readily be achieved.

In such instances, there is no alternative but to confront the patient tactfully with the evidence of his anger and its effects and to try consistently to enlist his aid in understanding and overcoming it sufficiently for treatment to proceed.

Although rapport between patient and therapist is an element crucial to the success of all forms of treatment, this does not mean that a therapeutic alliance is required in supportive psychotherapy. The therapeutic alliance, the working alliance, or other similar terms generally require the presence in the patient of an "experiencing ego"—an ability to report on his feelings and thoughts—and an "observing ego"—an ability to regard his own feelings and thoughts with some degree of distance and objectivity, and to comment on them. While such an "alliance" is not essential for successful supportive psychotherapy, it may become apparent to the therapist that the patient is demonstrating or developing a capacity for self-observation; when this does occur, it should be regarded as a strong suggestion that it is opportune to attempt to change the form of therapy from supportive to insight-oriented. At such a time it is useful for the therapist to maintain therapy in a "gray area," a form somewhat intermediate between the two forms of therapy, until it becomes clear, through successive steps towards insight, that the patient can actually tolerate and work in insight-oriented therapy. The shift from one form of therapy to another will be discussed in further detail in a later chapter.

Before beginning treatment, I recommend to patients in supportive therapy that they tell whatever thoughts or feelings are going through their minds during the hour. This may seem inappropriate because it is essentially the same as the "basic rule" recommended for patients in psychoanalysis and insight-oriented psychotherapy. It could lead the patient to associate too freely and permit the emergence into awareness of primitive thoughts, feelings, and primary process material, which would lead to further difficulties in maintaining an already fragile ego-defense system. While this is certainly a possibility, in practice it is most uncommon because the therapist does not pursue the associations and interprets neither resistances nor the content of the associations.

In the unusual circumstances that the patient's associations

should begin to lead him into areas which provoke intense anxiety, these associations can effectively be limited by an "upward"
interpretation, that is, by focusing the patient's attention on specific, current life events, or alternatively by suggesting that the
patient suppress—that is, consciously try to put out of his
mind—the particular thoughts, memories, or fantasies that are
eliciting the anxiety. The value in allowing the patient to report
on what "is in his mind" is that, if thoughts and feelings are
already in awareness, nothing is served by prohibiting or deter-
ring the patient from speaking of them openly with the therapist,
nor will eliciting these thoughts cause them to become more destructive. In fact, it is generally useful for patients to tell the
therapist what they are thinking so that the therapist is aware of
what is preoccupying them. It is the only way in which he may
deal with it. Only when the therapist knows of the patient's bizarre, delusional or hallucinatory thoughts, or his feelings and
impressions, can he work with them. This is not possible if the
therapist, for whatever reason, does not encourage the patient to
speak openly. Furthermore, the patient is relieved to be able to
ventilate these frightening, shameful, or guilt-provoking thoughts
with someone else, in an atmosphere of respect and compassion.
When, however, the therapist finds that the patient is repeating
this material over and over, he can tactfully suggest that it no
longer serves any useful purpose to continue to report it and can
put it aside.

An additional and important potential advantage in allowing
the patient to air his thoughts is that despite the most careful
evaluation it is possible that the patient is, in fact, more suitable
for and capable of tolerating insight-oriented psychotherapy than
the therapist had previously suspected. In such situations one
may begin to see that the patient is more or less freely associating
with no more than tolerable anxiety; there may also be evidence
that he is able to utilize some observing ego.

The patient should be encouraged not only to communicate his
thoughts and feelings during the hour, but to describe in some
detail what his life is like on the "outside," that is, in between
the therapeutic interviews. The therapist should have a fairly clear
picture of what the patient does, thinks, and feels when he is not
in his presence. It is surprising how little some therapists actually

know about their patients' lives. It is especially important with patients in supportive psychotherapy that the therapist know what kind of work the patient does; what he does when he comes home from work (or does he have one or several drinks at a bar before he reaches home?); how he spends his evenings; his eating, drinking, and drug habits, if any; his relationships with both the people at work and members of his family; his friendships; his leisure time activities; what he does on his weekends; his sexual behavior—if the patient is able to talk somewhat freely about it.

One cannot depend on the patient to report this material and, if it is not spontaneously forthcoming, the therapist should make appropriate inquiries. A lengthy interrogation is not required, but I do propose that the therapist should progressively develop a well-rounded picture of his patient as a person living and working in a specific milieu. This kind of knowledge is useful in any form of psychotherapy, but I believe it is particularly valuable in supportive psychotherapy, i.e., when working with patients whose lives are apt to be ungratifying and constricted or destructive to themselves or others. Although the kind of life a patient leads derives, to a large extent, from his psychological makeup or set, his behavior tends to reinforce that set. Human beings regularly behave in ways that support and strengthen the inner mainsprings of that behavior. When they experience their lives with satisfaction, the dynamic interplay between external behavior and psyche enriches them. However, when the psychological set gives rise to painful, maladaptive behavior, creating a vicious circle of impulse and reinforcement, then it behooves the therapist to attempt to break the cycle. It is usually faster and easier to do so by effecting some change in the external behavior than by modifying the inner set.

Joyce K., now 28 years old, had been previously married and divorced. She had been verbally, sexually, and at times physically abused by her father, and later by a stepfather. Her numerous sexual relationships were almost conscious attempts to find the "good father." However, on a deeper level more removed from awareness, there was a need to relive, and so to finally conquer, the pain inflicted on her by her sadistic fathers. As a result, she had an uncanny knack of becoming enmeshed with men who, despite charming appearances, were exploitative and abusive.

Each such experience merely strengthened the underlying trauma and impelled her to seek yet another cruel relationship to master. She was like a losing gambler who attempts to recoup her losses by raising her successive bets.

Information about a patient's daily life is important to the therapist not only to round out his understanding of the patient but also to demonstrate to the patient that the therapist is working with him. It can also serve as a valuable barometer of the patient's overall psychological and social equilibrium. It can provide the therapist with the opportunity to moderate behavior which is not in the patient's best interest or to foster behavior which is adaptive and moves the patient in directions which he himself desires.

In a related way, it is often necessary in supportive psychotherapy for the therapist to meet with members of the patient's family, or at least to have some telephone contact with them. This is a delicate problem because even though it is often essential to enlist the cooperation of the family when one is treating a particularly disturbed and often suicidal patient, one must maintain a strong rapport with the patient, who should feel that the therapist is working with *him*, as *his* ally. The patient should not be led into thinking that he is "sharing" the therapist with other members of his family. Such contacts with family members, and under special circumstances with close friends, classmates, or colleagues, may at times be vital for the well-being of the patient, but must be handled with careful attention to and consideration of the patient's thoughts and feelings relative to these contacts. The patient should be consulted about the importance of a particular contact, and his approval should be obtained in all but those situations in which he is possibly suicidal, homicidal, or genuinely unable to understand the situation. This approval should not be merely a formality; the therapist should ascertain if it is truly given freely, without significant ambivalence, and is clearly understood.

If the patient flatly refuses to permit the therapist to consult with other individuals, the reasons for the consultation should again be discussed in order to persuade him of the importance of such meetings. However, if he persists in opposing communication between his therapist and the other individuals, then the therapist should feel bound, in most situations, to respect the patient's wishes, and to avoid doing what is likely to severely jeopardize rapport with the patient. Exceptions exist, as mentioned above, but it is of little avail if the therapist rides roughshod over the patient's wishes by communicating with the family only to have the patient refuse to see him any longer. As with most similar problems in supportive psychotherapy, the emphasis must be on flexibility, empathy, and the protection of the therapeutic relationship.

For many patients, beginning treatment is very often an experience akin to entering a haven. They may experience it as a "holding experience," a situation described by Winnicott (1963) and Modell (1976), in which he has the conviction that he is being protected and cared for by the therapist. If such a feeling does not exist, it should be the therapist's initial goal to establish such a conviction in the patient by his careful attention to meeting his appointments on time and with regularity, his rigorously nonjudgmental posture, his empathic attitude, his respect for the patient, and his own relative freedom from anxiety when he is with the patient. Such a conviction of being "held" is, of course illusory, since the therapist cannot, in reality, protect the patient from all of his potential destructiveness, and certainly not from the "slings and arrows" from the outside world. However, he can demonstrate his willingness to help him work towards a more harmonious inner life and a better adaptation to the world around him.

4

Goals of Treatment

The goals of treatment should be identified, at least in the therapist's mind, in all forms of psychotherapy. In supportive treatment, they should be agreed upon by both patient and therapist, particularly since so often the patient has difficulty in articulating his reasons for seeking treatment. The failure to establish goals is one of the most common pitfalls in supportive psychotherapy.

In an earlier chapter, supportive psychotherapy was characterized as a "substitutive" form of treatment, and so it is reasonable to assume that either the patient will, at some point, no longer need the substitution from the outside, or he will continue to do so for an indefinite period of time. The therapist should, therefore, determine fairly early in treatment whether supportive psychotherapy might be terminated after some relatively identifiable period of time, or whether it is likely that lifelong "supplies" will need to be given. A decision, once made, can be changed, but it is invaluable for the therapist to have a sense of direction in this matter; otherwise, supportive psychotherapy may meander aimlessly, go on indefinitely and unnecessarily, or be terminated prematurely.

Although we often hear dire warnings about the danger of inadvertently stripping a patient of his defenses, and thereby precipitating a psychotic episode, it is my impression that the unnecessary prolongation of psychotherapy is a much more common problem. In the optimal supportive treatment, the stated goals will, to some extent, be achieved by the therapist's support of acutely or chronically deficient mental functions; he will provide the opportunity for the patient to ventilate his problems and painful feelings; he may recommend changes in the patient's external life, which can range from hospitalization to helping him obtain work, vocational rehabilitation, etc. He may assist the patient to clarify maladaptive patterns in his behavior; he may use suggestions, prescribe medication, and work with family members.

In contrast, in insight-oriented psychotherapy, the broad strategy is to help the patient gain a greater understanding of himself, particularly in regard to the focal conflicts and problems which have brought him to treatment. In this type of treatment, the therapist hopes to achieve a reduction of conflict, a shift in the organization of the patient's defenses, from one which is less adaptable toward one which is more adaptable, and establishment of new, more enriching identifications. Again, it should be stressed that both types of psychotherapy rarely exist in pure forms.

THE AUXILIARY EGO AND SUPEREGO

The psychotherapist's work in supportive psychotherapy can be described as providing the patient with an *auxiliary* ego and superego. Thus, in dealing with maladaptive ego functions, he attempts to diminish the most pathologic defense patterns of the patient while encouraging healthier defenses such as repression, reaction formation, intellectualization, and rationalization; he may attempt to modify a rigid and punitive superego by "giving permission" for behavior which the patient's overly harsh standards have prohibited; conversely, he may try to strengthen a patient's own control over socially unacceptable behavior by showing him how this results in painful feelings of guilt and leads to self-punitive behavior. Like a good parent, he can give permission for drive discharge in appropriate ways which are acceptable to both the patient and to his milieu, and he may help him limit such gratifications when they are excessive or inappropriate. The psychotherapist's goal should, in fact, be similar to those of the patient, with perhaps the major difference that each conceptualizes and names the problems differently.

KEEPING GOALS FLEXIBLE

Not unusually, the goals that have been established at the outset of treatment may prove to be unrealistic, become unimportant to the patient, or be pushed to the background; they may even disappear entirely and other goals may come to dominate the patient's concerns. Miss Joyce C., a recent high-school graduate, was referred for therapy because of frequent, disabling headaches which kept her in bed for hours on end. After two months of treatment which was, in fact, an extended evaluation, the purpose of which was to decide what form of therapy would be appropriate for her, the therapist realized that she had not spoken about her headaches for several weeks. Instead, she began to talk about her father who had died suddenly two years earlier. It gradually became clear that the patient was suffering from a prolonged and "pathologic" grief reaction and that her headaches were symptomatic of that condition. Therapy increasingly became explorative, and significant progress was made in overcoming Miss C.'s pathologic mourning. Just before termination, some 10 months later, the patient recalled that her headaches had begun to disappear when she had started to talk about her father.

KEEPING THE TOTAL PICTURE IN MIND

The psychotherapist always needs to be alert to such changes as Miss C.'s and to what the patient's overriding preoccupations are at any given time. Both patient and psychotherapist can lose the forest for the trees by narrowly and relentlessly focusing on a specific problem while overlooking another significant area currently in the patient's life which requires attention. Because of this concern, in supportive psychotherapy the therapist should maintain a reasonably good idea of how the patient is functioning at work, at home, in his relations with the people around him, and in any other areas that might cast light on his current psychological status.

Arnold T., a 35-year-old electrician, was referred to a clinic by his family physician who correctly believed Mr. T. was depressed. In the initial interviews, Mr. T. focused on his difficulties with his employer. Appropriately, the therapist worked to help Mr. T.

understand his part in the problems he was encountering at work. But at the same time, unknown to the therapist, the patient's marriage was rapidly falling apart. Before Mr. T. and the psychotherapist could even begin to explore the problems at home, his wife had left him. He had simply been too anxious about his home situation to discuss it in treatment, and the therapist had failed to inquire. One cannot depend on the patient to provide the therapist with an ongoing picture of his life; tactful inquiries should be made at appropriate times about the various areas in the patient's life, especially those about which he has been particularly reticent.

INITIAL VAGUENESS OF GOALS

At times psychotherapy, whether it be insight-oriented or supportive, may begin without an explicit understanding of goals because the patient's complaints are so vague and his description of what he wants to achieve is so unclear that goals simply cannot be established. In these situations it is useful to clearly identify this vagueness so that the therapist and patient can agree that one of the primary aims, if not the principal aim in the early phase of treatment, would be to establish, if at all possible, a specific goal. This is particularly important with patients who complain of suffering from feelings of being "out of things" and "feeling alienated," of malaise, loneliness, feelings of emptiness, and other pervasive moods and emotions which seem unrelated to specific life events. Narcissistic patients, borderline patients, and some patients with hysterical personalities, among other types, frequently express themselves in such diffuse, impressionistic, and fuzzy terms, that they make the establishment of goals extremely difficult and often impossible. If goals cannot be established, therapy should begin in any case. Usually the issues become clear as patient and therapist work together.

Patient's vs. Therapist's Goals

Unfortunately, a clear goal or goals in treatment does not always correspond to the wishes of the patient but rather to what an over-zealous therapist thinks is appropriate. The goals may primarily represent certain values of the psychotherapist which he is consciously or unconsciously foisting on the patient. Although it would seem self-evident, it is always essential to determine just what the patient himself wants from therapy. The therapist should always ask the patient not only what led to his coming to treatment, but just what specific help he wants from the psychotherapist. It is not rare to find that such basic questions have never been asked of a patient. Sometimes the patient has come merely for the renewal of a prescription of some new medication. He may be seeking referral to a medical clinic, or may need a letter for a legal purpose. Also, at times, the patient may use the visit to a psychotherapist merely as a means of dealing with a home situation which has gotten out of hand. Some patients may agree to psychotherapy for a variety of reasons which have nothing to do with psychotherapy as such; i.e., they may agree to come because they feel too embarrassed to refuse what their family doctor has recommended; or they may agree because they hope that the therapeutic relationship in itself will help them achieve some other goal in life; or it may be used to influence someone in their environment.

Therapists may also recommend psychotherapy for reasons that have more to do with their own needs than those of the patient, and they may find themselves agreeing to goals desired by the patient which are highly unrealistic; in these cases, they may allow themselves to be swayed by the patient's deep yearning for help, his mental anguish, or his ability to charm the therapist. It is true that in the not very long run the inappropriate setting of such goals becomes apparent; this may not have any long-lasting, harmful effects on a patient, but it may prove to be painful to him because his hopes have been raised by the therapist's validation of them, only to have them crushed. As in most matters of this sort, such "killing with kindness" should always suggest that there are countertransference issues at play and the therapist should, accordingly, carefully examine his own thoughts and feelings. The matter of countertransference will be discussed in a later chapter.

THE "HOLDING" ENVIRONMENT

As suggested in the previous chapter, supportive psychotherapy, no less and perhaps more than other forms of psychotherapy, provides a "holding environment" for the patient. The "protection" here resonating with early emotional ties with the mother and other important "caretakers" in childhood serves against both external dangers and the patient's own impulses. In supportive psychotherapy, the therapist can point out external dangers when the patient himself is unable to recognize them; he can also serve as a benevolent, limit-setting parent when the patient's own impulses threaten to erupt.

In contrast to insight-oriented psychotherapy, in supportive treatment it is incumbent upon the therapist to be explicit and direct, when the occasion demands it, about his attitude towards his patient's destructive impulses. It is not enough merely to explore with the patient the psychodynamics of his behavior and its effects; it is important to try and limit destructive impulses as best as one can. The therapist should identify destructive acts for what they are and inform the patient that he, the psychotherapist, is personally concerned about such behavior and its ultimate emotional and material impact on the patient. If necessary, the patient should be told that uncontrolled behavior during the therapy hour, for instance, cannot be permitted. However, rather than simply prohibiting such behavior, the therapist should help the patient recognize that it has a particular meaning and represents a form of communication even though it is dangerous, possibly destructive, and certainly ineffective.

In a similar vein, the therapist can inform the patient that he cannot carry out the treatment unless the patient cooperates in certain specific ways such as: taking necessary medication, attending Alcoholics Anonymous meetings, not engaging in certain antisocial behavior, etc. Again, in contrast to insight-oriented psychotherapy where the stress is on insight, here the goal is one of correction, or rehabilitation. These issues are extremely difficult to deal with because it makes little sense to punish a patient for the very symptoms which have led him to seek treatment. On the other hand, the continuation of such behavior can lead to a stalemate in treatment. The only path open to the psychotherapist is to repeatedly and continuously attempt to engage the patient in a struggle against his destructive impulses while at the same time pointing out, at a level within the patient's grasp, why he continues to engage in this behavior. In addition, the therapist should attempt to guide the patient towards substitutive activities which can give him gratification and pleasure which in turn will tend to diminish the need for the maladaptive acts he had been carrying out.

These tactics are far from simple and require long-term efforts to bring about even modest changes. However, surprisingly, at times, the patient may change much more rapidly than expected. In any event, genuine changes and useful modifications are possible and enhance the gratification of the psychotherapist from this kind of work.

5

Qualifications of the Therapist

In most clinics and inpatient services, supportive psychotherapy is usually carried out by the least experienced members of the staff, such as psychiatric residents, social worker trainees, younger psychiatric nurses, psychology interns, and medical students. Furthermore, these individuals may do it reluctantly and regard it as a monotonous and ungratifying chore, since they see the lack of interest in supportive therapy among more senior staff members. Like most human activities, supportive psychotherapy, when practiced with attention paid only to the superficial aspects of the problems rather than to the deeper dynamic issues at stake, can readily become a boring task.

PSYCHODYNAMIC TRAINING

Far from being an intellectually and emotionally undemanding form of psychotherapy, supportive treatment requires a therapist with a firm grounding in the principles of psychodynamic psychiatry. However, because of the nature of supportive psychotherapy, a trainee can effectively practice it if he is under the supervision of someone who does possess the appropriate experience and skills. With good supervision, a conscientious and devoted trainee can do effective work. Since the primary task of the therapist is to support such psychologic functions as are acutely or chronically deficient, it follows that his work remains firmly in the domain of what is in the patient's consciousness or, to some extent, what is at the edge of awareness, that is, in his preconscious. Interpretations of unconscious material are not made except under exceptional circumstances.

The ability to make such interpretations is not, therefore, a requirement of the therapist doing supportive therapy. On the other hand, he must have a good working knowledge of the patient's psychodynamics precisely so that he will not erroneously make interpretations which could weaken a patient's already failing ego defenses; one of his goals, in fact, is to strengthen those adaptive defenses. The therapist's strategy and tactics in supportive psychotherapy, as in all forms of psychotherapy, include not only what he should do but what he should be careful to avoid.

WORKING WITH DIFFERENT TYPES OF PATIENTS

The qualifications of the therapist who wishes to do supportive psychotherapy are not limited to his experience and understanding of psychodynamic principles as they may be applied to this form of treatment. It also requires an emotional and characterological posture that enables him to work with these patients. They are often individuals who have previously had relatively severe psychiatric problems and even psychotic episodes. They include patients with severe character disturbances; they may have limited verbal ability although their levels of intelligence are variable, high as well as quite low. In general, they do not engage the therapist in the kind of human interaction that is more characteristic of patients in insight-oriented psychotherapy. In insight-oriented psychotherapy there is, optimally, a reverberatory process in which transference reactions, interpretations, the emergence of corroborative memories and other associations, occur in a wider matrix in which this material and resistances are interpreted, thereby permitting the emergence of new material. This entire perspective, which is the bedrock of insight therapy, is not present for the most part in supportive work. Consequently, the therapist may feel much less drawn to practice it. If his response is to become anxious, excessively frustrated, bored, or lonely, he should seriously consider if he is able to work at that time with these patients.

Because of their more severe psychological disturbances the patients in supportive psychotherapy may be particularly prone to act out their feelings both in and out of the treatment hour; they may be uncooperative and even overtly hostile, to the extent that they may actually frighten the therapist by threats of physical violence to him, themselves, or others. Initially, they may be so intensely depressed that any verbal exchange is markedly limited, making the therapist feel helpless in assisting them. On the other hand, they may be floridly delusional, agitated, or manic.

Paranoid patients, in particular, present a special problem because of their profound lack of trust in the therapist and their well-exercised ability to evoke intense realistic and countertransferential reactions of rage, revenge, and aversion.

In a somewhat similar way, those narcissistic patients, who because of other criteria are not appropriate candidates for insight-oriented treatments, will often be extremely trying to the therapist because of the way they relate to him. Because of the combination of narcissistic and "borderline" traits, they have the propensity, perhaps even more than patients in insight therapy, to bring about what may at times be intolerable countertransference feelings; such reactions will be discussed in more detail in a later chapter.

Because of the foregoing difficulties, a therapist who is beginning to do supportive psychotherapy should do so, at first, to a limited extent, only expanding these activities when he feels comfortable in doing so.

The "Infantile" Patient

There are certain patients with whom, from previous experience, a therapist knows he cannot work well, and it is wiser, in such situations, that he not attempt to treat these individuals. For example, the intensely voracious, oral-dependent, demanding, infantile patient who chiefly seeks some form of "mothering" can quickly become an immense burden, especially to a therapist who cannot tolerate such unrelenting demands. He may react abrasively, and even by attempts to indirectly cause the patient to leave him; or he may react to his hostile feelings by being overly attentive and "kind" to the patient, thereby limiting the patient's self-growth and maturity, at least within the limits of his potentialities.

Mrs. Roberta A., a 44-year-old divorcee, was first seen in consultation when she was hospitalized for essential hypertension of several years' duration. The consultation was requested because the nurses on Mrs. A.'s medical ward were complaining about her continuous demands on them. She demanded attention, asked for special foods and off-ward privileges, and frequently insisted that the resident, who was her primary physician, be called so that she could tell him how shabbily she was being treated. The psychiatric resident, who interviewed her for his consultation visit, was impressed with her verbal ability and her intelligence (both perceptions were correct) and believed she would be a good patient for insight-oriented psychotherapy.

The patient was transferred to an open psychiatric ward where she began therapy, three times a week, with the psychiatric resident. At first, she was voluble and seductive, expressing her pleasure at having been able to leave the medical unit, but soon her demanding behavior began anew. She made inappropriate demands for special favors not only from the nursing staff and her therapist, but also from every other resident on the ward.

Her doctor initially gratified these wishes, but soon realized that the more he gave the more she demanded. Mrs. A. tried to stay in bed most of the day, bitterly fought off all attempts to engage her in occupational or recreational activities, and used meetings of the therapeutic community to berate the staff for their "incompetency" and "laziness." Finally, it was discovered that she had been secretly breaking her diet and buying food in the hospital snack bar; she had gained twelve pounds and her blood pressure had risen significantly.

When her therapist, who felt responsible for these developments, confronted Mrs. A. with her behavior, she turned on him, telling him that he was just like her former husband—"an egotistical idiot." From this point on, the patient did not stop provoking and disparaging him and he felt totally victimized by the patient for whom he had initially had high expectations. Despite supervisory help, it soon became apparent that the therapist could no longer work with Mrs. A., and transfer to another resident was arranged. Not only did this patient have a lifelong history of such behavior, but the resident also recognized, subsequently, that he himself had considerable difficulty in tolerating relationships in which the other person regarded him in anything but a respectful, if not admiring light.

Other Problematic Patients

A chronically depressed patient, who is barely communicative, intolerant of all attempts to mobilize him, and yet complains that "nothing is being done" to help him, is another type of patient whose behavior may lead to strong countertransferences. The group of patients described as having a "borderline personality," who excessively resort to "splitting"—see others and themselves as all good or all bad—launch hostile attacks on the therapist, are at times unable to control their sexual impulses, and may become an intolerable burden to some therapists. Although some of these particular problems, as mentioned earlier, will be dealt with in detail in a later chapter, the principal issue here is that every therapist should not necessarily consider himself as able to treat all patients in supportive psychotherapy or, for that matter, in any other form of treatment which he practices. Above all it is important for him to be aware of the patients that he can work with as well as those for whom he cannot be genuinely helpful.

ANALYSIS FOR THE THERAPIST

In this regard, the question must be raised whether every therapist should routinely undergo psychotherapy or psychoanalysis if he himself wishes to practice psychotherapy. Although this issue is discussed from time to time with no conclusion generally being reached, it remains a matter of first importance. Obviously, for individuals in psychoanalytic training, personal analysis is a basic requirement; the question then pertains to those therapists who do not enter psychoanalytic training. Although I know of no pertinent documentation to support my point of view, I believe that if a psychotherapist desires to work with patients in any form of psychotherapy based on psychoanalytic principles, it seems necessary that he should have an optimal grasp of his own unconscious processes.

Since countertransference reactions are an inevitable part of all forms of psychotherapy, and since they can either enhance the therapist's understanding of his patient or become a destructive element in treatment, it is essential that the therapist learn to recognize his countertransference attitudes. Since countertransference as an unconscious process cannot be recognized directly, it must be identified through its derivatives; it is, therefore, evident that the therapist must have a reasonably good idea of his own psychological makeup in order to be able to recognize these derivatives, minimize their effect on his work, and at the same time utilize them whenever possible to deepen his understanding of the patient. If, in fact, he is able to do so without having had personal psychotherapy or psychoanalysis, then such treatments are unnecessary. However, in my experience, the individual who has reached an adequate insight into his own makeup without having had personal therapy is exceedingly rare. I myself have never met one.

For those who are doing psychotherapy, it is certainly possible that, with many patients, personal therapy or analysis of the therapist, although desirable, may not be necessary. Nevertheless, every therapist should strive for a deeper insight into himself, especially when he finds aspects of himself intruding into his work. As far as understanding the patient is concerned, this, of course, will be developed through didactic teaching, reading, and supervision of his work with specific patients.

LIMITING THE NUMBER OF PATIENTS

Despite the best preparation or aptitude of a therapist for supportive psychotherapy, I would suggest that the therapist should limit judiciously the number of patients he sees in this type of therapy. Each therapist has to discover what his own limits are and stay within them. The practice of psychotherapy should be interesting and gratifying to the therapist, and he should feel no obligation either to practice all forms of therapy or to work with all types of patients. While he should be careful to be reasonably certain that his decisions are not stereotypical reactions, stemming from his own neurotic conflicts or character problems, he is a free agent whose work can be flawed when it is not carried out willingly and with enthusiasm. It is not beneficial to a patient to be treated by a therapist who only reluctantly works with him; it is far better that the therapist arrange for a colleague to see the patient and that he limit himself to those individuals with whom he feels more comfortable.

SUPERVISION OF SUPPORTIVE PSYCHOTHERAPY

The particular qualities of supportive psychotherapy and the qualifications of the therapist as have been described create a situation that makes it possible for a special organization of supervision to take place. An effective arrangement, which unfortunately is rarely used, consists in having an experienced therapist supervise a group of several beginning therapists who are doing supportive psychotherapy. Since outpatient supportive psychotherapy often requires the patient to be seen on a relatively infrequent basis, perhaps once every two to four weeks, or even as infrequently as once every several months, and because the duration of visits may be short (20 to 30 minutes), it is possible for a given therapist to see a fairly large number of patients in supportive treatment. For example, if one therapist sees an outpatient for 30 minutes once a month, he can follow eight different patients by spending only one hour a week doing supportive psychotherapy. If five such therapists meet as a group with their supervisor, that supervisor can supervise the treatment of about 40 patients in supportive psychotherapy in one hour a week. Such group supervision can deal both with general issues pertaining to supportive psychotherapy and to fundamental psychodynamic principles, as well as with specific problems relating to the patients who are being treated by the trainee therapists.

It seems that only through such an arrangement can the immense need for well-supervised supportive psychotherapy be met in a reasonably adequate manner. That this or other appropriate ways of dealing with the problem of adequately treating patients in need of supportive psychotherapy has not been undertaken is both disappointing and puzzling. However, regardless of the reasons for this situation, it is one that can be corrected, and a great deal of useful service can be rendered to the large population of patients who need supportive psychotherapy.

6

Behavior of the Therapist

The role of the therapist in supportive psychotherapy is in many respects different from that in insight-oriented psychotherapy. In insight-oriented psychotherapy, similar to psychoanalysis, minimal intervention by the therapist permits the patient more freely to express his thoughts, feelings and fantasies without the pressure or distortion of external stimuli, cues, suggestions, or any form of guidance. The therapist is *neutral* (that is, does not impose his values on the patient), relatively anonymous, and empathic, while monitoring his countertransference reactions; these conditions foster a desirable and controlled regression in the patient which is obviously inappropriate for already regressed patients or for those who, for any reason, either cannot benefit from such regression or react too intensely to it. The conditions of silence and relative anonymity specifically encourage the development of a regressive transference, a process which also is generally to be avoided in supportive psychotherapy. (Regression used here covers two situations: one concerns the retreat to an early level of sexual development—usually to some time in an individual's life when he was caught up in intense conflict and overwhelming feelings; the other area of regression reflects a retreat to earlier modes of mental functioning—this may relate to ego defenses, cognitive functioning, etc.)

THE "FRIENDLY" RELATIONSHIP

It is my impression that the form of patient-therapist interaction which is most useful in supportive treatment superficially resembles a social relationship but fundamentally differs from it in that the therapist specifically directs his comments towards certain therapeutic goals. This procedure is not without potential pitfalls because the therapeutic relationship can become one which not only has the outward form of social discourse but which is also like it in content, to the neglect of therapeutic goals. The *friendly* relationship, which permits the therapist to function as an agent of support, would then be transformed into a relationship of *friendship* in which the auxiliary role of the therapist is lost.

Many observers have noted that some psychoanalysts, whose work is regarded as competent in the practice of classical psychoanalysis, function less appropriately when they are engaged in analytically oriented psychotherapy; at such times, it seems, especially when doing supportive psychotherapy, they do not have in mind an identified model of what they are aiming for; they have not clearly conceptualized their interventions and the impact these might have on the patient. They may develop an ambiguous relationship with the patient in which the goal of treatment either is suffused in a vaguely social relationship or vacillates between that and a more analytic posture.

Schafer (1974) dealt with this issue when describing "how to talk to patients," based on his experience doing psychoanalytically oriented psychotherapy with college students. The "pedagogical and personal" approach he used seems especially appropriate in supportive psychotherapy. By "pedagogic" Schafer meant the appropriate sharing of the therapist's knowledge about the patient. By talking to the patient "personally," Schafer meant that the psychotherapist tries to cast his comments in a language which does not set him apart from the patient's concerns and which empathically relates him to those concerns. While such a "personal" approach is appropriate in all forms of psychotherapy, it is indispensable in supportive treatment where the patient's tolerance of frustration is usually significantly lower than in patients seen in insight-oriented psychotherapy.

It is useful for the therapist to engage in some small amount of social conversation with the patient at the beginning or ending of the hour or even during the hour if the occasion should arise in a natural way. Similarly, the patient's curiosity about the therapist's personal life can be satisfied to some extent, when that knowledge specifically is recognized by the psychotherapist as potentially useful in furthering the course of treatment.

For example, a female patient who had had several schizophrenic episodes, and in whom the therapist had begun to see evidence of a developing positive transference, inquired whether he was married. Without questioning her as to what might have led her to wonder about it, he replied that he was married. This simple piece of reality was helpful in dampening her growing erotic transference. Certainly, it did not totally negate it, but it did have a muting effect. Had the therapist not been married, and had he so informed his patient, it might have fostered the transference; in such a situation it would perhaps be wiser for him not to respond directly to the question, but to answer by noting that he doesn't think such information is especially useful to the patient and that, instead, they should focus on the current problems the patient is encountering.

When questioned by the patient, the therapist may not only acknowledge, for example, that he is married and has children, but he may tell the patient about some activity that he was engaged in during the previous weekend or during a vacation; and he should feel relatively free to give his opinion about certain issues if he believes that doing so will strengthen his rapport with the patient. It is clearly not to the patient's benefit if the therapist engages in political, social, religious, or any other kind of ongoing debate with him; nor should the therapist persist in protracted discussions on issues about which they disagree. However, the therapist should feel free to show his interest in such issues when this will enhance a sense of being and working together.

HELPING THE PATIENT MAKE DECISIONS

Rather than concentrating primarily on understanding why a patient requests specific guidance on a problem in his life, as would be appropriate in insight-oriented psychotherapy, in supportive treatment the therapist may actively help the patient come to a decision if the patient is genuinely unable to do so himself; in this way, the therapist can serve as an "auxiliary ego." In such situations, the therapist can, for example, help identify the possible paths open toward the resolution of a problem; he can help the patient put to one side those alternatives which are unrealistic or unworkable; and he can directly guide the patient toward a particular solution to a problem. However, the therapist should provide only as much assistance as is necessary; the patient should always be encouraged to try and make decisions on his own. Above all, the therapist should not become an overcontrolling parent—he should not present himself as an omniscient oracle.

VALUE JUDGMENTS

The therapist should also be as careful and scrupulous as possible to avoid injecting his values into such decision making. One often hears the criticism that therapists cannot avoid introducing their own ethical values into treatment. Curiously, in the name of candor and honesty, some of these critics often demand that the therapist overtly introduce his particular set of values; needless to add, those should be the same as those of the critic.

It is true that the possibility of influencing a patient is always present, but as with other temptations in life, one must deal with it by first recognizing that it may exist, then recognizing when it actually is occurring, and trying, as best as one can, to control the temptation. Optimally, a patient should be helped to make his own decisions and to carry them out regardless of the therapist's value judgment of them. If the decision is not self-destructive, not emotionally or socially harmful, and may in fact lead to a greater stability and an enhanced psychological harmony for the patient, then it is appropriate for the therapist to support it. Admittedly, one might quibble over what is meant by "socially harmful"; but for the most part such ambiguities can be resolved on the basis of common sense, at least in a vast number of cases.

When a patient characterizes the people in his life—past or present—in strongly judgmental ways, it may at times be useful and even necessary for the therapist to validate the patient's opinion of these individuals. For example, if a patient who often has trouble evaluating what he sees describes a particularly sa-

distic individual in his environment, who apparently is responsible for the patient's distress at the time, he may need to hear
the therapist's opinion and support for his own perceptions. Although there is room for distortion in such reports by patients,
this possibility can be dealt with simply by telling the patient,
"If what you say is generally correct, then it would seem to me
that. . . ." or, "From what you tell me, it appears that. . . ." Such
interventions help the patient test reality better and may actually
assist him to reconsider his perceptions and opinions when he
hears the therapist's qualified support of them. If the therapist
either ignored the reality of these reports or, even worse, attempted to refute them, the patient might cling to them more
steadfastly, might experience the psychotherapist as unempathic,
or might become more confused about his own perceptions.

A TOUCH OF FRIENDSHIP

Many of the patients seen in supportive psychotherapy are
lonely people, whether or not they live alone or with other people,
and they have a need, in the most human sense of the word, for
another person. To some extent the therapist can be that "other
person" even within the limits of his functions as a psychotherapist. For many such patients, the weekly or monthly visit to the
psychotherapist represents the high point of that period, even if
a visit lasts only 20 to 30 minutes. It can be a warm and fulfilling
encounter in which the patient feels respected, when he experiences that someone who takes him seriously is interested in him
and his concerns, and when he may have no doubt about the
empathic quality of the therapist's response to him. Such responses must, of course, be genuine; otherwise, the patient will
quickly perceive that they are sham. Even if an individual has a
significant psychologic disturbance, by no stretch of the imagination should this lead one to conclude that he is not perceptive,
sensitive, and intelligent.

SUBLIMATION OF SEXUAL AND AGGRESSIVE DRIVES

There is a broad scope in supportive psychotherapy for helping
the patient find sublimatory channels for sexual and aggressive

drives which cannot be dealt with or gratified in socially acceptable ways. Suggestions for sublimations, encouraging the patient to engage in them, and the exploration of possible, appropriate activities are a necessary part of the assistance the therapist can provide for many of the patients he may see in supportive psychotherapy. Even if the therapist's efforts seem to be unsuccessful, or only partially effective, he should maintain a steadfast position of encouraging the patient to involve himself in those activities which can gratify drive derivatives.

For example, a male schizophrenic patient in his mid-twenties, with strong, although unconscious, homosexual tendencies, was encouraged with some success to go out with women even though those encounters were expected to be, and indeed were, totally platonic. He found that he was able to ask women to go with him to movies or for walks, and he obtained a great deal of pleasure from the human contact as well as from the sense that he was a man associated with a woman; he felt this not only in his own eyes but reflected in the eyes of people around him. He felt reassured of his heterosexuality, and this reinforced his defenses against the rising fears that he might be a homosexual, fears which earlier had led to an episode of panic so intense that he had had to be hospitalized.

In the same way, patients with hostile, destructive urges can be directed towards specific behavior that can siphon off some of their aggressive impulses. Sports, hiking, gardening, and other fatiguing activities can be very beneficial and, among other things, help induce sleep. Many patients find considerable pleasure and increased self-esteem through dance, art, music, and other forms of artistic expression even if it is not designated as "art therapy" or "dance therapy." It is useful even if they experience these activities as spectators, but it is obviously more so if they are participants. Of course, when appropriately carried out, formally structured art and dance therapy can be extraordinarily beneficial for some patients.

COUNSELING THE PATIENT

There are many occasions during the course of supportive psychotherapy when actual counseling of the patient is indicated.

Under the proper circumstances, that is, when a patient himself is unable to deal with a situation, one can help with suggestions regarding difficult relationships with individuals in his environment, or in respect to his social activities, or about his work. To some degree, many patients in supportive psychotherapy have difficulty in understanding other people and in grasping the impact they themselves make on the people around them. Their own inappropriate behavior may lead them into difficulties with these individuals. One consequence of this is that they often permit themselves to be used and abused by others because they lack a sureness about how and when to resist such abuse, or because of underlying needs to be submissive or masochistic.

The counsel offered by a therapist should not be given in an authoritarian fashion but can be presented informally, with the stated and avowed purpose of simply helping to guide the patient. The use of introductory phrases such as "have you ever thought that you might. . . ." or, "in similar circumstances people have found it useful to. . . ," can be helpful. It is not unusual for the therapist to attempt to give some structure to the therapy hour and to the external environment of the patient as well. Bibring (1953) calls such tactics "manipulation." This may take the form of conveying to the patient the therapist's expectation that he come to his sessions regularly and on time; that he is responsible for the financial arrangements; that he is expected to try and put his thoughts and feelings into words; that he cannot behave in an unruly or violent fashion in the therapist's office.

HOSPITALIZATION

Manipulation also relates to the therapist's need to talk with members of the patient's family, to prescribe medication, and to adjust the therapy hours when necessary. The most drastic form of manipulation is to have the patient enter (or reenter) the hospital. Depending on the circumstances, this may be voluntary hospitalization; when the patient is overtly suicidal or homicidal, and refuses hospitalization, involuntary commitment should be carried out. Patients who need to be hospitalized from time to time should be taught to become sensitive to the subtle, progressive changes in them which tend to precede the necessity for hospitalization. In this way more intensive interventions or very early hospitalizations may be carried out; generally speaking, the earlier a patient enters the hospital, the shorter his stay will be. The patient can be educated to recognize the prodromata of an impending breakdown so that the prompt initiation of inpatient treatment can be accomplished.

Randolph K., a middle-aged research scientist, had suffered many episodes of manic-depressive illness prior to the use of lithium. Even before the availability of lithium treatment, he had learned to identify his feelings and behavior that presaged an episode of mania or depression. His psychiatrist, whom he had seen on and off for over 15 years, had carefully "collected" the various subtle symptoms that preceded Mr. K.'s episodes of mania or depression and had repeatedly reviewed these with the patient. Mr. K.'s ability to anticipate severe mood alterations had reached a point when his hospital stays were as brief as one week, and hospitalization was often not even necessary because of adjustment of his medication and/or brief psychotherapy focused on current precipitating events.

Supportive psychotherapy with the hospitalized patient will be discussed further in a subsequent chapter; at this point, suffice it to say that therapy with these patients is unfortunately too often a hodgepodge treatment with goals, strategy, and tactics that are insufficiently delineated by the therapist or his supervisor.

OTHER COUNSELING

Another form of "manipulation" may consist of counseling and suggestions regarding living and occupational arrangements: whether the patient should leave or return to his family; job changes or other employment-related issues; leisure time activities, etc. Work with other employment-related people in the patient's environment may become essential, and here the greatest flexibility should be used so that all possible arrangements for meeting with family members may be considered: meetings of the entire family with or without the patient, or with particularly important individuals, such as a spouse or parent, again with or without the patient, etc. These and many other combinations should all be considered, and the most useful and appropriate format adopted.

CHANCE MEETINGS

As may occur with any patient, the therapist may, by chance, meet a patient he is seeing in supportive psychotherapy outside of the therapy hour. In such situations, it is natural for the therapist to be more cordial to the patient, more of a "real" person, than he might be with a patient he was treating in insight-oriented psychotherapy. In the course of such encounters it is useful for the therapist to ask after the patient's well-being, much as if he were an acquaintance. It is important that the patient see the therapist as a socially adaptive individual who does not behave in what he might otherwise perceive as a bizarre manner, but who is comfortable in social situations. This does not mean that the patient and therapist should enter into lengthy and intimate conversations, but simply that the greeting should take place in a natural and unstilted manner in which the normal amenities are preserved. The therapist should always bear in mind that patients in supportive psychotherapy, like all patients, tend to identify with certain aspects of their therapist. With patients in supportive psychotherapy, such identifications may be fostered, especially when they pertain to such fundamental matters as social adaptation, sublimatory activities, etc.

SETTING LIMITS

Not infrequently the therapist must set specific limits to the patient's behavior both in and out of the therapy hour. It is impossible to establish a simple rule to identify the behavior which should be dealt with by setting limits; a useful rule of thumb is to support all behavior which can be regarded as mature and adaptive and to discourage all behavior which seems to be in the service of regression, immaturity, and maladaptation.

For behavior which is clearly regressive and which occurs *within* the therapy hour itself, the therapist should make clear to the patient that such activities are not appropriate in that particular setting. For example, a young female "borderline patient" was frequently given to barely disguised, masturbatory behavior within the hour. Although the therapist was loath to confront the patient with this activity, he finally did so in a tactful and gradual way. In this way, he was later able to point out that such behavior was not "wrong" in itself, but that it should be carried out privately rather than in the therapist's office where the time could be used more profitably to look at the patient's current problems. The patient was also told that perhaps such behavior was her way of communicating something to her doctor which she was otherwise unable to articulate. When she admitted that this was so, the therapist encouraged her to try and put her thoughts and feelings into words so that he could better understand what she was thinking.

This raises the question of asking about embarrassing or apparently abhorrent matters. Even the most delicate matter can be broached to a patient in supportive psychotherapy if the issue is approached in a "step-wise" manner. In that way, if an overly intense reaction begins to develop, the therapist can modulate or put a brake on his intervention.

In the same way, behavior outside of the hour may also require some discussion and limit setting. A young unmarried woman developed the habit of "cruising" singles bars almost every night. Since these were places where there was a strong possibility that she might be physically hurt, this activity was discussed with the patient in terms of its realistically self-destructive potential. In these discussions, the therapist took the opportunity of tactfully confronting the patient with the contradiction between what she said and what she did, and to some degree he offered a clarification of impulses of which she was almost aware. Clarifications of this sort tend also to give the patient a plausible explanation as to why he feels or behaves in a particular way. Thus, at the very least, such clarifications and "interpretations" can provide the patient with the useful defenses of intellectualization and rationalization of his behavior, thus diminishing his anxiety or guilt. At the same time that these defenses are supported, the patient can be shown how they can be utilized in subsequent situations.

THE FLEXIBLE APPROACH

These examples are typical of how supportive psychotherapy demands a most flexible approach and how the therapist must constantly be guided by his consideration of what will promote growth in the patient and what will prevent regression. These considerations should take precedence over any "rules" or regulations concerning therapeutic interventions. For example, a patient who lives at a considerable distance from the nearest therapist or who, because of agoraphobia or illness, is unable to come to the therapist's office may effectively be helped by arranging for periodic phone calls. These can be arranged to take place at specific times and for a fixed duration; the fee can be established beforehand, perhaps approximating that for an office visit of equivalent duration. It may even on occasion be necessary for the therapist to work with someone in the patient's family who comes to see the therapist in place of the patient.

Peter A., a young adult schizophrenic, had rarely left his parents' home for many years and flatly refused to see a psychotherapist. In desperation, the parents consulted a therapist for help in dealing with their son's progressively increasing aggressiveness. Over several years, during which time the patient's parents were counseled once or twice a year, they were able to lead their son towards some increased self-reliance; this enabled him to leave the house more frequently, to stay by himself while they were away, and to take some responsibility for his own financial arrangements. They were able to set useful limits on Peter's potential for aggression and often managed to interest him in outside activities. Obviously this is not an optimal form of treatment but its utility is evident.

THE THERAPIST'S LANGUAGE

Since all forms of psychotherapy largely depend on verbal communication, the therapist's language becomes a critical instrument. This is probably even more significant in supportive psychotherapy because the therapist runs a greater risk of being misunderstood by his patient. His language should be as clear and concise as possible. Lengthy interventions will lose the patient in the verbiage. To the extent of his ability, the therapist should try to use pungent or vivid language since it not only has a strong impact but has a greater chance of sticking in the patient's memory. "Your behavior tends to be self-destructive" is a clear and concise statement but, "you often spit in your own soup" or "you seem to burn your bridges before you even get to them" express the same idea but possess a saltiness that the first comment lacks. When using such figures of speech, the therapist should be reasonably sure that the patient grasps the intended meaning, rather than taking the metaphor literally.

Language that refers to sexual matters, defecation, sexual relations, etc. should generally not be street language, even if the patient himself uses "four letter words." When the therapist uses those words, he does not truly know how the patient hears them. They may strike him as patronizing, seductive, or as attempts by the therapist to show that he is a "regular guy." Patients usually do not expect the therapist to use the same language as they do. On the other hand, if a conventional, nontechnical word or phrase can be found, that is preferable to using a polysyllabic word. Above all, whatever language is used, one should be reasonably sure that it is fully understood by the patient.

Many patients in psychotherapy consciously and unconsciously hide their thoughts and feelings behind vague and inexact words or psychological jargon. The therapist who is not sure what the patient is saying should always tactfully ask him to explain what he means. If a patient says he felt paranoid, one can say, "People use that word in different ways. Tell me a bit about what you mean by it." This helps the patient to clarify his own thoughts and identify his feelings. If the therapist works toward this end, he can do no better than to set an example for the patient by his own language.

Humor can be a firecracker. At its best, humor can make a point with impact, conciseness, and a powerful sense of having quickly grasped an idea. Unfortunately, it also lends itself to destructive uses—it can be biting, sarcastic (literally: tearing of flesh), and is a common way of thinly masking hostility, narcissism, and exhibitionism. The worst of it is that the humorist usually is unaware of his hostility and how it is embodied in the joke. Kubie (1971) was fairly adamant that the therapist should avoid humor altogether. I feel it has a place but, just as with any other intervention, the therapist should know why he is using it and how it is probably affecting the patient. Objection may be raised that this self-consciousness concerning humor destroys spontaneity. That may be a consequence, but it is preferable to stifle some spontaneity than either to hurt the patient or to show disrespect for him.

In these matters, as in everything the therapist does and in the way he thinks about the patient, the guiding concept is that he should conscientiously avoid stereotypical "therapeutic" behavior, but should feel free to do what he believes will further the therapeutic process—in short, be of help to the patient. Mindless spontaneity and a rigid adherence to rules are opposite sides of the same coin—they ignore the patient's needs. Flexibility to meet the situation must be the guiding concept. Once a therapist systematically begins to focus on the patient's needs, on his specific weaknesses—and strengths, therapy usually begins to progress satisfactorily.

7

Strategy and Tactics

The minimum goal in supportive psychotherapy, and the overall strategy which should be aimed towards its achievement, is to keep the patient from psychological deterioration or to limit its extent if it does occur. With many of the patients seen in supportive psychotherapy, transitory regressions will occur, and special measures, such as the use of psychotropic medication or hospitalization, must be taken. However, apart from preventing these relatively limited setbacks, the therapist can broadly aim towards several rehabilitative goals. Perhaps the most important is to help the patient to live a life which is more comfortable in that it is as free as possible from frequent, intense, and long-lasting episodes of psychological suffering: intense anxiety, depression, irrational oppressive guilt, humiliation, and self-depreciation.

DEALING WITH RELATIONSHIPS

The patient's relationships with people are usually the principal sources of his misery. For example, he may make impossible demands on others and repetitiously conjure up expectations that cannot be fulfilled. To a large extent, these are transference reactions—that is, inappropriate reactions to people as if they were significant individuals in the patient's early years. When his idol topples from the pedestal on which it has been placed, the patient is disappointed, sad, and possibly filled with hatred. Guilt over his destructive wishes often leads to depression as he sees himself as worthless. The patient has to be shown, concretely, in situation after situation, over a long period of time, how he contributes to the erosion of his relationships.

Characteristically, since the patient disclaims responsibility for the chaos into which his relationships fall, the therapist must tactfully and repeatedly confront him with his part in the sequence of events.

REALITY AND DISTORTION

The same sort of confusion often reigns over the patient's work or school commitment. Over and over, he angrily reports on painful, confused, humiliating situations, ignoring his role in provoking or worsening them. He often sees himself as an embattled victim at the mercy of his family, teachers, employer, or society as a whole. The therapist must carefully attempt to differentiate reality from distortion in these accounts because he cannot assume that all of the patient's difficulties are the product of his disturbed perceptions. For example, it is only too likely that a patient in supportive psychotherapy comes from, or still lives with, a chaotic family. In such circumstances, as mentioned in the previous chapter, it is important for the patient, who may have doubts about his own assessment of the reality, to hear his perceptions validated by the therapist. To maintain an abstract "neutrality" in the face of a family's destructive behavior towards a patient is to ally oneself with that family and against the patient. On the other hand, one must avoid falling into a gullible acceptance of everything the patient reports. When appropriate the therapist can give a qualified agreement by saying, for example, "If the things you tell me are basically like that, it must have been very painful for you, etc., etc. . . ." I have given other types of responses in Chapter VI.

ENHANCING ADAPTATION

Another way of describing the strategy of supportive psychotherapy is in terms of the need to enhance the patient's ability for adaptation: first in relation to his internal milieu—his impulses, conscience, defenses, conflicts, fears, etc.; and secondly, in relation to the external world. It might be said that such a view advocates that patients "conform" to their society. In a narrow sense this criticism may seem justified, but more correctly the adaptation toward which I propose that the therapist work relates to a recognition of the *realities* of the external world, not of its values. How the patient feels and what he does, if anything, when he has correctly understood his external environment is quite different from, and clearly preferable to, behavior based on a grossly distorted view of external reality.

In supportive therapy, as in all psychotherapy, the possibility of imposing one's values on the patient is always present. As noted in an earlier discussion of this matter, the most useful approach is to be aware of the possibilities and to do one's best to resist the impulse to impose one's values, overtly or covertly, on the patient.

TECHNICAL APPROACHES

A comprehensive classification and conceptualization of the "technical" and "curative" procedures, or principles, used in various psychotherapies was developed by Bibring (1954). It is the technical aspect of these procedures that is relevant to this discussion on tactics. Bibring's five procedures, in summary, consist of:

1. *Suggestion.* This relates to the "induction of ideas, impulses, emotions, actions, etc., in brief, various mental processes by the therapist (an individual in authoritative position) in the patient (an individual in dependent position) independent of, or to the exclusion of, the latter's rational or critical (realistic) thinking." Suggestion is frequently combined with hypnosis in a curative as well as in a technical sense. In supportive psychotherapy, the therapist may use suggestion to tell a patient that a particular symptom will disappear, or that the patient will be able to return to work or be able to utilize previously (hysterically) "paralyzed" muscles. In these examples, suggestion is not only a technical intervention, but may be "curative" of symptoms.

2. *Abreaction* has been used with a number of different mean-

ings. When originally described by Breuer and Freud (1893), abreaction was regarded as a process which permitted repressed, unconscious emotions to be discharged in a normal way, rather than to be expressed through symptoms. I use it here, more simply, to mean the discharge of pent-up emotions, whether these have been conscious or not. This can serve the purpose of permitting the patient, in a supportive environment, to give vent to long unexpressed, intense feelings which he may have been afraid or ashamed to express. This is often followed by considerable subjective relief. Not infrequently, the patient has not even been aware that he is sitting on a "volcano" of emotions.

For example, Mrs. Heather M., an intelligent, attractive, 50-year-old housewife, was admitted to a medical service for investigation of numerous thoracic aches and pains which she had experienced for almost a year. The interview soon established that Mrs. M. was deeply resentful of her husband's overinvolvement in myriad activities and that, although he was considerate of her when they were together, he usually was not home. When the interviewer "wondered" how Mrs. M. handled her husband's nightly absences, she began to sob and finally, in no uncertain terms, expressed her bitter anger with Mr. M. She avowed that not only had she not shared her feelings with anyone, but that she herself had been relatively unaware of them. It was clear that she was afraid to be aware of her anger—and other feelings—toward her husband. Recognition of her feelings about his neglect opened up the possibility of counseling which helped Mrs. M. deal with her problems.

3. *Manipulation,* a term which Bibring acknowledged to be unsatisfactory, "covers a wide field of therapeutic measures." Though he recognized that some of these are not curative, and so dismissed them from consideration, such techniques are particularly appropriate in supportive psychotherapy. Under this heading are counseling, advice, guidance, limit setting, prohibitions, and encouragement of specific behavior, such as facing a phobic situation, or discussion about some specific behavior. It encompasses environmental manipulation such as hospitalization, changing the frequency and duration of therapy hours to deal with transference, the prescription of psychotropic medication, interviews with family members, etc. Manipulation also in-

cludes symptom and defense "substitutions" such as a mild obsessional thought for a hostile fantasy, or the encouragement of more adaptive defenses such as intellectualization, rationalization, reaction formation, or suppression in place of projection, denial, and splitting.

4. *Clarification* is made of psychological material which is in or close to being in awareness. It defines those interventions of the therapist which reflect back to the patient his thoughts, feelings, behavior, attitudes, etc., of which he has perhaps been aware, but in a vague and disconnected manner. Thus, with Mrs. M. above, the interviewer helped to make her aware that her vague feelings of distress represented anger and sadness about her husband's neglect. Another patient who was constantly abusing her child was shown that she was displacing her anger from her divorced husband on to her child. All sorts of maladaptive behavior patterns can be demonstrated to a patient. In supportive psychotherapy such clarifications are limited only by the extent of the patient's psychological-mindedness and motivation for understanding and change.

Confrontation, of which Bibring does not speak, seems to be subsumed under clarification, but is also a form of manipulation since it characteristically, and by design, tends to evoke anxiety. Although it can be used in appropriate situations with selected patients, care must be taken that the patient can tolerate the degree of anxiety evoked. Until the patient and therapist have developed a solid therapeutic relationship, and the therapist has begun to have a good sense of his patient's psychological strengths and weaknesses, it is best for him not to use confrontation.

5. *Interpretation* is the final technical and curative principle. This procedure, by definition, relates to those statements the therapist makes with specific reference to unconscious material and which go beyond the apparent clinical data; they are psychoanalytically informed inductions based on, but going beyond, what the therapist has learned from the clinical material. The use of interpretations may provoke intense feelings of anxiety, sadness, humiliation, etc., as well as cause the patient to relive painful periods in his past. They should be reserved for the patient with a reasonably well-developed ego who is in insight-oriented psychotherapy or psychoanalysis.

REPETITION IN THERAPY

In the course of this chapter, and often throughout this book, I have used the word "repeatedly" many times. I believe that repetition in psychotherapy is central to one's success. Beginning psychotherapists sometimes cherish the illusion that once they have made a clarification or interpretation, the patient will not only understand it right off, but will integrate that insight into the fabric of his personality. Unfortunately, that rarely, if ever, happens. Any given piece of insight represents a terrain that must again and again be fought for, lost, and recaptured. Maladaptive behaviors—character traits for the most part—are deeply ingrained and have served the patient in many ways, to deal with a variety of situations, and for many years—usually since childhood. As a result, they require "repeated" discussion. However, it is useful for a therapist to find different ways of saying the same thing. Nothing sounds more nagging to a patient—as to all of us—than to be always told the same thing in the same way, especially when it is something he does not want to hear.

CONFRONTING REALITY

Tactically, the therapist must, above all, place himself on the side of reality. Although he cannot challenge each and every distortion the patient utters, in any given phase of treatment he should confront the patient's principal error in reality testing. Whereas in insight-oriented psychotherapy the therapist would focus on the underlying dynamic reasons for the patient's misperceptions, in supportive work he will generally limit himself to correcting the error itself. Typically, such distortions appear in the form of reality-blurring defenses. Although it is true that all ego defenses say no to some piece of reality in the patient or in his environment, there is a considerable difference in the maladaptiveness of using projection, for example, as compared to the potentially socially adaptive utilization of reaction formation.

Head-on confrontations of reality distortions often strengthen the patient's mistaken view and pit him against his therapist. Confrontations of a less direct nature which are perceived as less abrasive by the patient can take the form of more or less rhetorical questions such as: "Perhaps your (spouse) had another motive for saying that (acting in that way)"; "Is it possible that you contributed, in some way, to this situation?" etc. If the patient vehemently reasserts the correctness of his view, it is pointless to be drawn into a battle over "who is right." I have found that the best approach is for the therapist to acknowledge that he himself "could be mistaken. If this occurs again, perhaps we'll be able to understand it better." If the patient sees that the therapist is not determined to be "right at all costs," "to win," his own defenses will tend to be less inflexible. Moreover, it is important that he should see the therapist's flexibility and reasonableness in the hope that he may, at least partially, identify with such an ability to bend, change and adapt.

ERRORS OF PERCEPTION

With certain critical errors of misperception, it is useful for the therapist to point out that although the patient may be correct, there is no way that the patient can really be sure. For example, when the patient states, without any evidence, that someone "has it in for him," he can be challenged by the comment that it is difficult to know what someone else is thinking or feeling. Sometimes the patient is at least partly correct, or his feelings are somewhat justified; it is then helpful to acknowledge the reality of the correct part of the perception while at the same time pointing out the incorrect aspect, or the inappropriate intensity of the patient's feelings.

PAINFUL FEELINGS

The patient who often finds his painful feelings absolutely intolerable usually has not developed a sense of the self-limiting nature of much psychological suffering. Like a small child, when he hurts he wants the sufferings to vanish instantly. I believe that this is what causes parents to suffer so much when their child is in pain. They know how futile it is to reason with a child, to point out that he will feel better soon, etc. If possible, the therapist can remind his patient of earlier episodes of stress, and remind him how they did abate over a period of time. He can show the patient how much his suffering is intensified when he hopelessly experiences it as a pain that will never come to an end.

If the therapist communicates his empathic response to the patient's pain, conveys his appreciation of what the patient is going through, most patients will more readily accept the therapist's comments that most pain diminishes in time. The therapist may also be able to counsel the patient as to what he might do to ease his suffering; this can take the form of work or leisure time activities. In appropriate situations, the therapist can suggest that if the pain does become intolerable it can to some extent be dealt with by the use of psychotropic medication.

IMPULSE CONTROL

When poor impulse control has been a prominent aspect of the patient's emotional and social difficulties, the therapist should promptly begin to deal with it, showing the patient that the resulting behavior is not in his best interest. He can be shown how such unreflective behavior creates trouble not only for himself, but also for those about whom he cares. The patient can be taught simple techniques of self-restraint; perhaps the simplest, at first, is for him literally to walk away from potentially destructive situations; often if he can take a walk, visit a friend, or go to a movie, the hostile impulses will abate. Such a suggestion can be coupled with the idea that the patient should hold off doing anything about his impulses until he has had a chance to talk it over with his therapist at their next meeting, if it is to occur fairly soon, or else he should telephone and discuss it then as well as arrange for a meeting.

When such a patient talks before acting, it is helpful for him to be told clearly that the therapist thinks well of his success in not carrying out the impulse. Then, together with the therapist, he can explore some other ways in which he might have expressed the feelings that gave rise to the impulse. If he has already acted inappropriately on the impulse, the exploration of an alternate way of dealing with his feelings should still be discussed since the patient may be able to utilize that alternative in the future. When the therapist discusses impulsive behavior after it has occurred, it is most important that he be especially careful not to be critical, punitive, or rejecting of the patient because of his behavior (even if the criticism is couched in subtle language). The patient has come for treatment because of his symptoms, one of which is his impulsiveness, and it is pointless to condemn him for it.

NONJUDGMENTAL ATTITUDES

The patient must recognize that the therapist is his ally in his attempts to deal with destructive behavior. In this sense, it is true, both the patient and the therapist are disappointed that a harmful impulse has been acted upon. However, if the therapist begins to judge such behavior from a moralistic point of view, he will jeopardize the therapeutic relationship and make it still more unlikely that some useful changes can occur; if he does it repeatedly, it is likely that the patient will stop coming for therapy. Perhaps worse, he may continue coming to therapy but will no longer report on anything he suspects will be judged harshly by the therapist and both patient and therapist will interminably enact a meaningless relationship.

Many patients have had considerable experience, in their formative years, of being nagged and criticized for their behavior by their parents, and over and over again they have been made to feel guilty or humiliated. When such feelings become chronic, they may lead to even more maladaptive behavior in a conscious or unconscious attempt to punish the parent who made them feel worthless. That is the situation which such a patient is apt to repeat with his therapist when the latter actually reacts parentally to behavior in which he believes the patient should not be engaging.

Sometimes such countertransference manifestations—for that is what such judgmental criticisms are—are provoked by ongoing situations in the therapist's own life which parallel events in the patient's life. Two of the commonest among these are marital difficulties and parent-adolescent conflicts. Although an uncontrolled countertransference may, for example, lead to punitive behavior by the therapist, he may also try to avoid such behavior by a reaction formation—that is, by being excessively kind to the patient—an attitude which is perhaps less painful (to both patient and therapist) but which does not contribute to the patient's welfare. The matter of countertransference will be dealt with more fully in the next chapter.

ENCOURAGING POSITIVE BEHAVIORS

One of the most difficult therapeutic tasks is to mobilize a patient to develop new, or to enhance existing, sublimatory behaviors. It is almost impossible for a therapist to encourage his patient to work or pursue some leisure time interest without seeming to put himself in the position of that same controlling, manipulative parent described above. In all such endeavors, the best course is to repeatedly, empathically, and firmly to point out to the patient that such (sublimatory) behavior is in his best interest. Indeed, nothing could be more true. In the first place, socially acceptable behavior serves as a derivative expression of sexual and aggressive drives. To the extent that the patient can engage in such activities, he will be expressing, releasing, and gratifying what are, for him, forbidden impulses. Moreover, such behavior cannot fail to have a beneficial effect on the patient's view of himself; he will actually be doing something which will strike a blow on behalf of his aspirations for his ideal self. Furthermore, it incidentally provides the therapist with a concrete example of the patient's potential which he can later point out as a genuine example of what he is actually capable; this can help refute the patient's long-standing cry of "I can't do it!"

It is startling and gratifying to see how a relatively small success in one area can have a progressively broader, positive impact on several areas of a patient's life. Constance N., a constricted, markedly underachieving college student was able to mobilize herself with encouragement from her therapist to commit herself more diligently to her work. Much to her pleasure and surprise, she was rewarded with several good grades. Her parents were no less delighted and, for the first time in years, they did not subject her to their usual semiannual post-examination scoldings. The patient was sufficiently elated that she was able to summon up courage to ask a young man she knew to a school dance, something she had never before been able to do. In therapy, she was less inhibited and began bit by bit to talk about some of her daydreams and her feelings about the therapist; she was beginning to act somewhat like a patient in insight-oriented rather than in supportive psychotherapy.

Unfortunately, such examples of the breakup of psychological "logjams" are not everyday occurrences; this one occurred after two and a half years of regular supportive therapy. I offer this vignette merely as a model of the potentially expanding ripple effect of supportive psychotherapy.

WORKING FROM THE PATIENT'S STRENGTHS

Again and again, one is brought back to the well worn, but nonetheless correct, clinical aphorism that one must work with the patient's strengths. There is no patient, regardless of diagnosis, who does not possess some strengths. The problem is to perceive them, and then to engage the patient in a commitment to utilize these more or less dormant qualities.

Such a mobilization of latent potentials is hampered by conflicts about success, long-standing inhibitions, fears of failure, profound needs to punish others by a continued marginal existence, etc. However, if some reasonable degree of positive rapport develops between the patient and therapist, he will not fail to see that his therapist wishes the best for him; then he may want to please this benevolent and caring parent by doing something he believes his therapist would appreciate. Despite frequent disclaimers to the contrary, to some extent every patient, even one who is quite regressed, appreciates the therapist's concerns and hopes for him. When the therapeutic relationship is strong, the patient will want to please his therapist. That is why all progressive efforts the patient makes, whether successful or not, should be acknowledged, and some appreciation of them conveyed to him.

8

Transference and Countertransference

Transference occupies a central position and is an impelling force in psychoanalysis and insight-oriented psychotherapy. It is the most powerful aspect of such treatment since it characteristically precipitates the patient's most intense emotions during the course of treatment. Consequently, it has an evocative and credible impact upon the patient. It is not an event that took place in the past or outside of the treatment hour; it is being lived at the moment, in the therapist's office, while the participants are actually present.

Transference consists of a displacement of feelings, attitudes, and fantasies that were originally experienced towards parents, siblings, or any other important individuals in the patient's early years, onto the therapist during psychotherapy or onto other individuals in the patient's life. Transference is such a ubiquitous human phenomenon that it is probably present in, and to some extent influences, all human relationships, especially those that are close and long-standing. Transference may occur even when the relationship between two people is slight and transitory. The patina it lends to all relationships cannot be considered pathological unless the transference feelings are so intense that they excessively subordinate the reality of the person toward whom they are directed. If a man desires maternal care from his wife or

she from him when one of them is sick, it is an appropriate transference regression. On the other hand, if the predominant character of the husband's attitude toward his wife is that of a son
toward a mother, it is obvious that the marriage may be in difficulty.

TRANSFERENCE IN PSYCHOTHERAPY

When intense transferences occur in the context of psychotherapy, they can become a stubborn impediment to the progress
of treatment: the patient is more interested in fulfilling his childhood wishes than in deepening his understanding of himself. In
this situation he is derivatively reenacting with the therapist a
relationship with some important person from his early years.
This then becomes the central focus of the therapist, who is able
to help the patient realize how his current life is distorted by the
past—by the child he once was and who still lives within him.

The therapist must work on two fronts: one, deal with the
transference as a resistance to treatment, and the other, work with
the transference as a distortion of current reality. Through a progressive process of clarification and interpretation, the therapist
demonstrates how the transference affects the therapeutic process
and how it influences the patient's adult life. Later, he identifies
the patient's transferences to him as displacements from the important people in the patient's life. The actual genesis of these
earlier attitudes may be explored. In a more or less lengthy phase
of "working through," the transference reactions are diminished
at least to the point at which the patient's experience of the therapist is only minimally influenced by transference. Through such
a resolution of the transferences, the patient also works through
the significant fixation points in his development. Because transference is the motive force in insight-oriented psychotherapy and
in psychoanalysis, it is essential that it be fostered in such therapy
in order to encourage the development of a regressive transference.

What facilitates the development of transference in psychotherapy is what has been variously described as the "opaque-
ness," "neutrality," or "anonymity" of the therapist. These terms
are generally taken to mean that the therapist remains a relatively

ill-defined individual for the patient; the patient knows little about him, although he obviously knows his appearance, the furnishings of his office, something about his feelings through the tone of his voice and gestures, etc. The more indistinct the therapist appears to the patient, the more it is possible for the patient to endow him with the characteristics that he had habitually observed in the important people in his childhood, and toward whom he developed enduring attitudes, feelings, and fantasies. Since greater contact between two people makes it more likely that the intimacy will lead one or both of them to reexperience the feelings they felt as small children (in a world of powerful adults), it stands to reason that frequent visits to a psychotherapist, who is identified as a helper, are apt to foster the transference.

Usually, in psychoanalysis and sometimes in psychoanalytic psychotherapy, the transference develops into a "transference neurosis." This is a reaction that substitutes, in effect, for the neurosis which originally led the patient to seek treatment. The therapist has become the individual onto whom all major childhood conflicts, usually centered on instinctual impulses and the prohibitions and defenses against them, are now displaced. The intensity of experiencing this "new neurosis," and its verisimilitude for the patient by virtue of its occurring as it does in the course of the treatment, make it an invaluable instrument for the interpretation, reconstruction, and working through of the patient's psychological difficulties.

When the therapist utilizes the transference or transference neurosis in insight-oriented psychotherapy, he has assumed that the patient is able to tolerate the reemergence of powerful, painful, primitive feelings and that he will be able to endure the frustration that must inevitably occur when his drive impulses are not gratified by the therapist. The therapist has also assumed that the patient who is experiencing these feelings and attitudes will be able to recognize that they are, in fact, inappropriate in the context of psychotherapy.

INAPPROPRIATE TRANSFERENCE

All of this is in marked contrast to the situation that prevails in supportive psychotherapy, in which the foregoing three assumptions are met in part or not at all: the therapist may believe that the patient is not able to develop such a transference or that if it does develop, the patient is not likely to be able to tolerate the frustration that lack of gratification entails, and finally, that the patient may not be able to maintain the dual view of his transferences which consists on the one hand, of experiencing them and, on the other, of recognizing their inappropriateness and illusory quality.

It may also happen that in a severely disturbed patient the transference may go on to develop, not into a transference *neurosis* but into a transference *psychosis* in which the therapist is not simply experienced as if he were, for example, a parent, but is actually *believed* to be that parent. Such a development announces to the therapist that the patient has lost an important part of his ability to test reality and has become frankly delusional.

AVOIDING TRANSFERENCE

It is therefore important for the therapist not to foster transference in patients in supportive psychotherapy, but rather to attempt to achieve a less intense state of positive rapport which, despite fluctuations during the course of treatment, will generally prevail throughout most of the time they are working together. If, despite the relative "reality" of the therapist and the infrequency of the patient's visits, a transference does begin to develop, it is clear that less anonymity and less frequent contact are indicated in order to establish greater reality and to create more emotional distance between the therapist and his patient. The therapist usually can regulate the amount of self-disclosure to enable the patient to see him as a clearly defined person. By controlling the frequency and duration of visits, the therapist can find a format that will balance necessary visits against formation of transference. If these steps are taken, the likelihood of a strong transference will diminish and what remains will be manageable.

Nevertheless, there is probably always some transference, and if changes in visits, etc., do not modify it, it should be dealt with directly by means of "upward interpretations," that is, by deliberately characterizing the transference feelings or behavior as a result of current, real situations, unrelated to early experiences in the patient's life. That is, they should be "interpreted" (more precisely *explained,* since an interpretation generally deals with unconscious material) in terms of something going on in the therapeutic situation at that particular moment or in the patient's current life outside of therapy.

For example, a patient who developed intense erotic feelings towards his therapist was told that such feelings seemed to represent his gratification that the therapist was working with him. If, despite all efforts, the transference reaches psychotic proportions, that is, if a transference psychosis begins to develop, the patient should, at a minimum, be placed on psychotropic medication if it has not already been prescribed, and hospitalization should be recommended in most cases.

COUNTERTRANSFERENCE

Countertransference is often a significant and arduous problem in supportive psychotherapy because the poor ego strength of many of the patients permits drive impulses of a sexual and especially of an aggressive nature to be expressed floridly. Patients in supportive psychotherapy are often unable to set their own limits and modulate or sublimate their drives, and so, not surprisingly, they tend to act upon their impulses toward the therapist. Among the many definitions of countertransference, I use the concept to mean the therapist's transference to the patient; in other words, a displacement of the *therapist's* attitude and feelings, originally developed towards important people in his early life, onto the *patient*.

To some extent, all of the thoughts, feelings, attitudes, fantasies, and dreams of the therapist that relate to the patient are influenced by his countertransference. There has been considerable discussion about the "real" reactions of patient to therapist and of therapist to patient, which some writers exclude from, or contrast with, "genuine" transference and countertransference reactions. As suggested earlier, this seems to be an arbitrary distinction, although it can be maintained in a limited sense, with some justification, if a fuller agreement between discussants exists. If one accepts the premise that no aspect of human behavior can exist in isolation from the rest of an individual's psychological makeup, then it must be assumed that to a *greater or lesser degree* the therapist's professional behavior also must be influenced by everything in *his* psychological makeup. The critical issue is the degree of interference in the therapist's professional tasks by the derivatives of his own inevitably incompletely resolved conflicts and by the intrusion of his character into his work. Such interference in a therapist's work, his intrusive countertransference, tends to be more intense when he works with severely disturbed patients. Therefore, it is apt to represent a greater problem in supportive psychotherapy.

PROBLEMS OF EMPATHY

In working with a patient in any form of psychotherapy, it is essential to be able empathically to identify with him in order to experience and understand what he is feeling. Countertransference is not the only cause of problems with empathy. Difficulties in identification with a patient may stem from a number of sources: the patient and therapist may come from drastically different social and cultural backgrounds; the patient may remind the therapist, consciously or unconsciously, of a disturbing individual in his past; and the degree of psychological disturbance in the patient may be so great that the therapist experiences him as a totally alien figure. The rapid and stormy transference reactions which a disturbed patient may demonstrate often create intense anxiety in the therapist, especially when associated with demands for immediate gratification of sexual impulses or a tendency to act on aggressive urges. Of course, there may also be general characterological problems in the therapist that prevent him from being effectively empathic.

The strain of experiencing countertransference feelings may lead to the therapist's markedly disliking a patient, even to the extent of wanting to retaliate for the patient's aggression. For example, the patient who taunts and threatens the therapist with his suicidal fantasies often evokes in the therapist a conscious or unconscious desire that the patient literally eliminate himself from the therapeutic situation. Some of the most severely disturbed patients seen in supportive psychotherapy can be extremely provocative, not only verbally but through their actions, especially through dangerous behavior both in and out of the therapy hour. They may plague the therapist with "unnecessary" phone calls to him and his family; therapy hours may be spent in total silence or in the enumeration of hypochondriacal complaints; abuse and threats of violence may fall on the therapist's head without his having any understanding of why. All of this leads to feelings of frustration, anger, impotence, and often a desire for retaliation.

UNREALISTIC GOALS

The degree of psychological disturbance in some patients creates a particular problem for the therapist whose therapeutic goals far exceed the possibilities of therapy for a particular patient. Such a therapist may want to "completely cure" the patient, "completely understand" him, and be warm, empathic and accepting of him at all times. Clearly these are unrealistic, utopian goals and usually lead to disillusionment and finally to a desire to reject the patient for what seems like a willful failure to cooperate with the goals the therapist had set for him. Moreover, it is difficult for a therapist to maintain his caring feelings for a patient who has a cold, provocative, and deprecating attitude towards him. The therapist may respond to his own anger with a reaction formation by being "overcaring," by feeling bored or anxious, by feeling totally inadequate to conduct the treatment, by denying his own feelings, or by denying the degree of the patient's psychological disturbance.

THE THERAPIST'S REACTIONS

Certain patients, in supportive as well as in insight psychotherapy, will tend to provoke specific countertransference reactions in the therapist. For example, masochistic patients will often evoke sadistic behavior in a therapist as a result of arousing feelings in him of hopelessness about his work. These patients may also make the therapist angry by denying that he has any caring or empathic feelings for them. Such patients can have a devastating effect on a therapist's self-esteem when they fling at him their feeling that he is a cruel, crass, humiliating, ungracious, and uncaring individual. The injury to a therapist's narcissistic aspirations may lead not only to anger but to painful feelings of guilt, shame, and depression. Narcissistic patients, because of their marked detachment from the therapist—a detachment which has been variously described as being in a cocoon or plastic bubble—often evoke feelings of boredom and sleepiness, sensations of fusion, feelings of indifference, and a general paucity of empathy.

Although countertransference is an inevitable occurrence, the core issue is the degree to which it interferes with the therapist's professional task. Despite the patient's behavior, the therapist must strive to maintain his empathic posture, to remain an experiencing, vulnerable (as opposed to rigid) individual, who has fantasies, dreams, impulses, and reactions to the patient, but who is able to be aware of them, to tolerate them, and to utilize them in enriching his understanding of the patient.

The guiding principle, then, is that countertransference should interfere minimally in the psychotherapist's work and simultaneously be a source of benefit and understanding to him. In this regard, the therapist must try to keep out of awareness—to suppress—events going on in his life which can intrude on his professional task: sickness at home, financial difficulties, his physical health, etc. Thoughts such as these are imperious and demand a hearing; however, it is not possible to dwell on them at length while one is doing psychotherapy.

THE THERAPIST'S PROBLEMS

Despite all attempts to understand and utilize one's countertransference reactions, whether they be primarily a product of one's own psychological makeup or whether they are primarily a reaction to the patient's behavior, these reactions may nevertheless disturb the therapist's psychotherapeutic work. In such a case, he should consider consultation with a colleague or perhaps refer the patient to someone else for continuing treatment. For the psychotherapist himself, the question of intensive psychotherapy or psychoanalysis is particularly indicated if he sees that his reactions tend to be habitual and even predictable when he works with certain patients. These reactions must be recognized amid the specific, transitory countertransference reactions which are responses to identifiable kinds of behavior by the patient—such as those described with masochistic or narcissistic patients. These countertransferences can be understood and utilized for the patient's benefit.

Some psychotherapists feel, because they themselves have undergone psychoanalysis or insight-oriented psychotherapy, that they will never again need further therapy. This is an unfortunate opinion because it tends to lock the therapist into a position of assuming that he is always correct and that difficulties in treatment always stem from the patient's psychological makeup. Freud's suggestion (1937) that an analyst "should periodically—at intervals of five years or so—submit himself to analysis once more, without feeling ashamed of taking this step" may be too sweeping for most therapists, but the spirit of the recommendation, if not the letter, is important. The uniqueness of every individual means that to some extent no two patients are exactly alike and, therefore, that each treatment is more or less different from every other. Every patient treated poses new problems, and new responses and insights are required, not only into the complexity of the patient's psyche, but into that of the therapist as well. In that way, learning to do psychotherapy is a lifelong task for the therapist who learns to look more insightfully into his patients and into himself.

The therapist who undertakes to do supportive psychotherapy is, in many respects, taking on a courageous task, for not only is it difficult to carry out, but it can be an emotionally arduous undertaking. Moreover, the intrinsic importance of such work is rarely appreciated and acknowledged by colleagues in the mental health professions.

9

Resistance

The classical psychoanalytic concept of resistance refers to a specific phenomenon that is encountered and systematically dealt with in psychoanalysis and psychoanalytically oriented insight psychotherapy. It refers to the conscious and unconscious responses in the patient that arise from significant disturbances in his psychological equilibrium and that are usually brought about by the therapist's request that he report everything going through his mind (free association). As the patient attempts to comply, he becomes aware of a tendency within him that pulls him away from speaking freely about what he is thinking and feeling.

Specifically, this resistance usually arises from the balance between sexual and aggressive impulses, the defenses against them, the demands of conscience, and the effects on these forces of external pressures or environmental stimuli of any kind. In psychoanalysis, where the patient is encouraged to freely associate, his thoughts tend to progress from those derivatives of the defended impulses which cause minimal anxiety to those which cause greater amounts of anxiety; the greater the awareness the patient has of these impulses, the greater his anxiety becomes.

Resistance, then, is intimately associated with anxiety and leads to both conscious and unconscious opposition to the treatment by one or more of a large number of mental and physical activities on the part of the patient. Not only may the patient utilize all of the well-known "defense mechanisms" such as isolation of affect, reaction formation, denial, undoing, etc., but he may use any piece of behavior which can restore the earlier neurotic equilibrium which had served defensively to keep the unconscious impulses out of awareness. For example, a patient may be silent or flood the hour with irrelevant matters. He may not remember any dreams or he may fill the hour with detailed dream reports to which he offers few or no associations. In this way, not only may a particular piece of behavior serve as a resistance but its opposite counterpart may serve the same function equally well.

In the course of psychoanalytic psychotherapy, a critical role is assigned to the clarification and interpretation of resistances in order to diminish their effectiveness. This is done principally by making them ego alien—consciously objectionable to the patient—in order that the unconscious impulses and the prohibitions against them may be brought into awareness. The therapist can closely follow the resulting anxiety that such interpretations evoke, and through his cognitive and empathic grasp of this process he can carefully control its intensity so that it is no greater than what the patient can tolerate. In fact, despite many anecdotes to the contrary, resistances are not usually so readily diminished as to leave the patient prey to an overwhelming episode of anxiety. Nevertheless, an estimation of the patient's ability to tolerate moderate levels of anxiety as well as other painful feelings is an important aspect of the evaluation of a patient for psychoanalysis or insight-oriented psychotherapy. A belief that a patient would probably be unable to handle a moderate degree of anxiety should tend to make a therapist disinclined to recommend insight-oriented therapy for that patient. Obviously, this is not the only criterion on which a recommendation for insight-oriented psychotherapy is based, but in the overall process of evaluation it is an important one.

RESISTANCE IN SUPPORTIVE PSYCHOTHERAPY

For patients who have been selected for supportive psychotherapy, the broad strategy explicitly precludes an attempt to diminish resistances in order to deal with the derivatives of unconscious impulses and their prohibitions. Given the premise that the patient in supportive psychotherapy is relatively unable to tolerate the anxiety that arises from a confrontation of his resistances, it follows that the therapist should not attempt to diminish their strength lest the patient's unconscious conflicts reach awareness and overwhelm him. Indeed, very often the therapist should attempt to foster these resistances; when unconscious impulses and fantasies threaten to flood the patient, and such defense mechanisms as he possesses seem to be increasingly failing, the therapist should bolster those defenses which seem to be most readily available.

In special circumstances, which will be described in a subsequent chapter, a cautious exploration of the area of resistance by "high level" interpretations may be attempted. However, most of the time, in supportive psychotherapy, resistances should be either left alone or enhanced when it appears that the patient's repressed thoughts and feelings threaten to emerge into full consciousness.

AVOIDANCE OF RAPPORT

Although the foregoing is an appropriate strategy, it requires a particular qualification when speaking of supportive psychotherapy because here "resistance" can be used to describe the avoidance of *any* rapport with the therapist, even when there has been no attempt to interpret the derivatives of unconscious material. In effect, the patient is resisting the supportive treatment itself for any one of a number of reasons which include such factors as: the ego syntonicity of his difficulties (they do not upset him), his need to hurt someone in his environment through his symptoms, his fear of the therapist, secondary gains from his symptoms, fear of change, etc. In these situations, the patient will indicate by his behavior or will verbalize his fear or reluctance to continue therapy. He may come progressively later and later to treatment hours, frequently miss hours altogether, or act out his fear or anger with the therapist during the hour. In all such situations, the patient's tacit communication relates to his need to avoid a therapeutic contact with the therapist and to flee from treatment. Sometimes a patient begins to develop a frightening transference to the therapist and the derivatives of these feelings and attitudes impel him toward behavior which in itself evokes anxiety and causes him to distance himself from the therapist.

Mr. Charles W., a 60-year-old married man, was initially being evaluated for a moderate depression. Later, he was found to be suffering from an early stage of Alzheimer's disease. During the evaluation, his underlying organic brain disease became increasingly evident, along with numerous areas of regression. In one particular session, he was obviously intensely anxious but was unable to explain what was upsetting him. During a subsequent remission, he was able to explain that he had had a powerful urge to perform fellatio on the interviewing therapist and had become very anxious when he thought he might reveal this impulse. During the remission, he was able to dismiss the impulse by regarding it, not altogether incorrectly, as due to his illness.

In such situations, as described in the chapter on transference, the therapist can make an "upward interpretation" or can let the patient control the frequency and duration of the visits which, in any event, should probably be decreased. If the duration of the sessions is shortened or the visits are spaced further apart, the patient should not be led to believe that such steps are punitive; on the contrary, it is useful if he himself participates in the decisions made about these matters.

UNDERSTANDING RESISTANCE

The first task of the therapist in dealing with resistance is to understand what it represents on a conscious and unconscious level for the patient. It is always a piece of dynamically important behavior and is potentially understandable even though the patient himself may not be able to work towards such understanding; he should not be encouraged to do so if, by exploring it, he might become severely regressed. The therapist may have to depend on his intuition to reach a tentative understanding of the resistant behavior. Regardless of the means by which he attempts to conceptualize the behavior, the therapist must deal with it, sometimes quite promptly, for not to do so would give it tacit approval, with the likelihood that the patient would leave therapy. Moreover, not confronting such behaviors, implicitly encourages the patient to *do* rather than to *reflect*.

With resistance, too, the *entire* situation must be considered: It is possible that with a passive or obsessive patient one might encourage some activity which could represent a progressive step away from rumination and fence-sitting. The therapist should initially ascertain if the patient's avoidance is conscious; if it is in awareness, he should be encouraged to discuss it, as candidly as possible, with the therapist. Very often resistance reflects transference attitudes, as mentioned above, which are usually erotic or hostile and which can be discussed. However, if the patient is unaware of the feelings or thoughts that prompt his resistant behavior, the therapist may be able to grasp the sense of these acts from the general flow of the patient's comments and be able to discuss his conjectures with the patient.

SETTING LIMITS

Other manifestations of resistance in supportive psychotherapy which weaken the rapport between patient and therapist, and which should also be dealt with, concern the setting of limits for behavior within the interview situation itself. This may concern threats of violence to the therapist, overtly seductive actions, masturbatory behavior, and behavior destructive of the office itself. It is essential that the therapist not permit such behavior, or else he will soon find himself in the position of having tacitly approved it. This is not only destructive of the treatment but can enhance pathologic tendencies in the patient. Furthermore, unless the therapist promptly deals with the behavior in a direct, nonpunitive manner, he will quickly discover that he is becoming angry with the patient and unable to work with him.

EXPLAINING THE PATIENT'S BEHAVIOR

Since many of the patients in supportive psychotherapy are often unable to work and communicate in the therapeutic situation, in the same way as patients in insight-oriented psychotherapy, the meaning of their behavior is often difficult to grasp; clarifications, as mentioned above, may then be based more on the therapist's intuition than on what he has perceived from the patient's material. However, it is useful tentatively, tactfully, and undogmatically to offer the patient a plausible and reasonable explanation of his behavior even if it is not very clear to the therapist. If accepted, this type of explanation can be used by the patient as an anxiety-binding intellectualization or rationalization. Resistances to therapy are derivatives of an unconscious conflict in the patient, and the therapist is in the difficult situation of attempting to deal with a clinical phenomenon which he is not able to fully explore because the patient is unable to cooperate. Nevertheless, explanations based on available material which is conscious, and so readily acknowledgeable by the patient, can be used effectively.

THE ROLE OF EGO DEFENSES

Ego defenses are complicated psychological phenomena which serve a variety of aims and evolve during the course of everyone's life. These formations have generally been conceptualized as "unconscious mechanisms" that primarily serve the purpose of dealing with aggressive and sexual impulses which would give rise to anxiety if they were to emerge in awareness or were acted upon. More recently, ego defenses have been regarded as phenomena with a variety of functions including, but extending beyond, the management of unconscious wishes. These functions include: gratification of all forms of pleasure, the avoidance of unpleasure in whatever form it occurs, and the support of general adaptive purposes. The organization of defensive processes in a given individual gives a particular stamp to his character or his personality. When particular personality traits are excessive and maladaptive in an individual, they are associated with "specific" character disorders which have been designated by such labels as: hysteric, obsessive-compulsive, paranoid, masochistic, etc.; these correspond to the most obvious aspect of the person's character; needless to say, many combinations of these disorders occur with varying emphases.

A patient in supportive psychotherapy often has been struggling to maintain the strength of his defense organization to avoid being overwhelmed by unconscious thoughts and the painful affects associated with them, principally anxiety. Because of the inadequate development of his ego or because of intense conflict or trauma, such a patient's defenses are not sufficiently able to protect him from the emergence into awareness of these painful feelings and thoughts. Therefore, in contrast to the attempt in insight-oriented psychotherapy to significantly diminish certain defenses and to generally modify the overall defense organization, the therapist's goal in supportive psychotherapy is specifically to strengthen these processes.

MALADAPTIVE EGO DEFENSES

It is clear, however, that certain defensive operations are far less adaptive, intrapsychically, socially, and interpersonally, than others. As a result, those defenses which are characteristically more destructive or maladaptive must be dealt with because, when chronically used by the patient, they lead to social and psychological disturbances. They are destructive of adaptational efforts since they conflict with reality testing and relationships with other people. Defenses such as projection and denial, when frequently used by the patient, are the most maladaptive, precisely because they so greatly distort reality. These defenses can be dealt with if one carefully attempts to demonstrate to the patient just how they undermine his best interests.

If repeated attempts to modify these pathologic defenses are unsuccessful, one may attempt to limit their use in other ways. For example, an elderly man, as a result of his growing cerebral dysfunction consequent to organic disease, was becoming increasingly paranoid. He believed that his neighbors were passing toxic and poisonous gases into his apartment through the ventilating system. Almost every day he complained to the police, who were becoming increasingly irritated with him and finally threatened to commit him. The psychiatrist to whom he was brought attempted to deal rationally with the patient's suspicions, but failed. He then told the patient that since other people, such as his relatives and the police, did not seem to understand him, there was little point in his speaking with them about his fears; instead, the therapist proposed that he should bring his concerns to him and he would be glad to discuss them with him. The patient asked the therapist if he agreed with him that he was indeed being threatened by his neighbors; the therapist replied that he was unable to really know because he didn't have enough information, but that he was certainly willing to listen to the patient and to try to understand the things that were upsetting him.

The patient returned once a week for a visit of about 20 minutes and each time described what his neighbors were doing to him. After eight or ten visits, he became less and less interested in relating the same stories and of his own accord decided to come for treatment only when he felt "upset." Subsequently, he described how he talked to himself and had imaginary arguments with his neighbors; he no longer argued with them or went to the police, and he lived quietly by himself, looking forward to visits from his children and grandchildren.

SPLITTING

Splitting, the inability to experience others—or oneself—as having both good and bad aspects, is another common defense found among the more severely disturbed patients. Although everyone probably "splits" from time to time, some individuals do it much more frequently, more exaggeratedly, and with less awareness of what they are doing than do others. They alternately idealize and deprecate the individuals around them; they have difficulty in remembering that the individual against whom they are raging at this moment is someone whom they had regarded as helpful and caring only the day before.

If a therapist tolerates the patient's rage and refuses to fight or argue with him, the patient may see that the therapist is not in reality as hateful as he had experienced him, but is a human being who is generally decent and helpful although not without faults and certainly not perfect. Needless to say, such a change in view does not come about easily, but it can be achieved over a period of time.

RECOGNIZING RESISTANCES

Dealing with these particularly pathologic defenses becomes especially important when they tend to disrupt the therapeutic relationship. For example, the patient may incorrectly claim that the therapist dislikes him or has hostile intentions towards him. The therapist must then deal with this ineffective reality testing in order to safeguard the therapeutic relationship, which may be the only link the patient has to rationality; in fact, it may be all he has to maintain him in a position of some independence and to avoid hospitalization. In this regard, the patient should be encouraged to learn to recognize, identify, and name his feelings so that he can begin to grasp what he is experiencing, and what events have provoked these feelings.

If he can begin to recognize and avow his own hostility, for example, a patient will be better able to learn why he perceives his therapist or other people as hostile to him. Although these clarifications may seem simplistic, they can be appreciated and utilized by many patients. Clearly, merely stating them once is without effect. However, if reiterated in a variety of situations, over and over, with good humor and tact, the distortions of reality will often decrease in both frequency and intensity.

10

Typical Situations and Techniques:
Distortions of Reality

Once a therapist has assimilated the general principle of supportive psychotherapy described above, he will be prepared to treat patients in most diagnostic categories and will not need to learn special techniques to work with patients whose diagnoses differ. In contrast to the foregoing chapters, which, for the most part, deal with broad strategic issues, this chapter and the three that follow are mainly concerned with tactical applications of the general principles. The underlying major premise is that the patient selected for supportive psychotherapy is suffering from relatively significant defects or deficiencies in ego function, whether these be chronic ("structural") or acute (stress or crisis reactions).

DISTORTIONS OF REALITY

Perhaps the most important problem confronting the therapist concerns the patient's distortions of reality, including his inability to recognize what is inside himself—such as his feelings at any given moment—and what is in the world around him. Distortions of reality can take many different forms and vary widely in intensity. At the lower end of the spectrum are florid misperceptions such as hallucinations and delusions; at the upper end are illusions and mild and unwarranted suspiciousness. Distortions may be strictly perceptual, such as in hallucinations, or more "purely" psychological, as with defenses which, in one way or another, deny something about oneself or someone or something else.

Poor reality testing, when marked, makes adaptation difficult and often impossible; it can erode relationships, it can lead to debilitating anxiety—as when an individual lives in constant fear of disaster—or to depression; it can pervade and dominate the life of an individual. Consequently, it is of utmost importance that the therapist work to mitigate at least the most blatant of the patient's distortions. This is not merely a pedagogical approach that concerns the "correction" of these misperceptions; it must be based on the therapist's realization that the misperceptions possess a dynamic content.

Poor reality testing does not imply that some "perceptual apparatus" has become defective, unless the patient actually has organic brain disease. Every misperception stems from underlying intrapsychic conflict or deep-seated character structure. Defective reality testing is a defense, the purpose of which is to maintain some psychological equilibrium and prevent flooding by intensely painful thoughts or feelings such as anxiety or depression. Not perceiving or appreciating something in the external world is a way of keeping emotional pain at a tolerable level. In other words, perception is optimally an act free of conflict. We select among perceptions and put them in order of importance relative to some goal. When perception is conflict-free, this process functions smoothly; in contrast, selection among perceptions is askew when it is affected by issues that are irrelevant to the goal. It is important to distinguish here a sensory process—the organic taking in and registration of sense data—from the process of perception, which relates to what is actually in consciousness.

Since patients in supportive psychotherapy are not usually able to work towards a significant diminution of psychic conflict (which distorts their perceptions), the therapist must attempt to deal with their misperceptions on a "higher" level—that is, on the level of reality testing itself. This would entail, for example, showing the patient that he misperceives, explaining his misperception through "high level interpretation," dealing with the derivatives of the misperception, helping the patient to progressively accept some of the affected reality, and showing him that it is safe to "look reality in the face." Such management does not mean that all of the patient's misconceptions should be dealt with; many are best left alone. Those misperceptions which are most maladaptive and cause the patient and the people around him the most suffering are the ones to be worked with.

THE ACUTE PSYCHOTIC EPISODE

The most dramatic situation in which poor reality testing is manifested is in the acute phase of a psychotic episode. The management of such a patient typifies the very nature of supportive psychotherapy. In this phase, the patient is at the mercy of his drive impulses which consist largely of aggressive rather than sexual tendencies. The patient's overwhelmed ego supplies little or no restraint in the form of defensive measures. As a result, he becomes potentially harmful to himself and to others; at the very least, he may provoke intense fear in the people around him. His contact with reality is so fragmented that not only is he incapable of surviving in society, he often has lost the sense of his own identity.

The therapist must promptly supply the deficient internal controls through hospitalization, psychotropic medication, and such humane and carefully considered restrictions as will alleviate his suffering and prevent him from doing physical harm to himself or to those taking care of him.

Even at this stage the patient may be capable of developing an attachment—slight and volatile as it may be—with some individuals. The therapist who works with such a patient should bear in mind that no matter how psychotic the patient may be, there are islets of normality that should be sought, identified, and harnessed, if it is at all possible. Admittedly, in an acutely psychotic individual, such strengths are difficult to discern. If the therapist sees him frequently, briefly, and regularly, some connection may develop; when he begins to recover he may then recognize the therapist as someone who served as a helper. The ground is then favorable for him to develop a continuing attachment to his doctor.

During this time, the therapist should strive to develop as much rapport as possible with the patient through careful attention to his own empathic posture—as well as that of other staff members. He should repeatedly reinforce reality, as opposed to delusion, and attempt to begin to work with the patient to explore some of the more prominent precipitating events that led to his illness.

Delusions

One of the commonest forms of psychotic misperception is the delusion. Delusions have traditionally been regarded as false, fixed beliefs. However, in clinical practice delusions are seen on a continuum, with some being much less resistant to modification than others. Although I believe that delusions can be modified, it does not follow that the therapist can simply contradict them; this has long been recognized as quixotic at best. However, neither should the therapist agree with the patient's erroneous reorganization of reality. He can initially respond to the patient's delusory statements, for example, by saying: "I don't know enough about what you are telling me to agree with you or not. If you tell me more about it, it may help me to understand things better."

This comment is not a ploy. The therapist listens carefully, asks questions, and shows, in fact, that he is interested in learning more. If he is able to gain some insight into the dynamics of the patient's delusion, he may be able to deal with it in several ways; one of these might be to explain it to the patient in the form of an "upward interpretation."

A young woman, Mrs. Janet C., began to believe that her husband was having a love affair and that he and the other woman, Martha, were planning to kill her. In the hospital, Mrs. C. was afraid to eat the food served her for fear that her husband had poisoned it. One day, she said that she had seen Martha in the serving area. She asked her therapist whether he believed her or whether he, "like all the others, think I am crazy." He responded: "I don't know what you mean by 'crazy,' but I do know that you have been extremely frightened and you're having trouble with your thoughts."

Mrs. C., while not especially satisfied with this answer, was not hostile to the therapist. Over the next several weeks, the therapist's hypotheses that Mrs. C.'s paranoid delusions were a projection of her own hostility to her husband and, on a deeper level, may have been related to an unconscious homosexual interest in Martha were verified. In working with the therapist to piece together the events that led to the precipitation of her psychosis, the patient mentioned that she first became suspicious of her husband when she saw Martha, a neighbor, sunbathing. Her first thought was: "God, what a beautiful body she has!" She ruminated on this for about two days, slowly becoming more and more anxious; during this time, the idea occurred to her that Mr. C. must also be attracted to Martha. From that point, there was a rapid evolution of the delusion of the love affair, followed by delusions of persecution. At the same time that her intense anxiety over her own homosexual thoughts began to subside, the delusion "spread" to the extent that she came to believe "everyone" was helping her husband carry on his love affair and was in league with him to get her "out of the way." This led to a resurgence of her anxiety.

The dynamics of Mrs. C.'s delusion—a process which seemed to serve unconsciously to deny her hostility to her husband, to bind her anxiety, and to deny her homosexual desires—were not, of course, interpreted to her. Instead, the therapist focused on Mrs. C.'s envy of Martha's youth and her prettiness; he wondered aloud whether she was worried that her husband might not still be in love with her, etc. In short, he supported her denial of unconscious homosexual impulses without agreeing with her delusional "solution."

Hallucinations

Hallucinations, sensory experiences without external stimuli, likewise should not be considered unchangeable or pathognomonic of psychosis. For example, hallucinations often occur when healthy people are isolated for long periods of time. Captain Joshua Slocum described this in the course of his solitary trip around the world in a small boat. Some bereaved people hallucinate the presence of the dead relative. Visions, especially of a religious nature, commonly occur in certain cultures where they are tolerated and may even be fostered.

With a psychotic patient, the therapist should tactfully obtain as much information as possible about the hallucinations before he confronts them in any way. He should ask questions such as: "When does this occur?" "How long does it last?" "Does it remind you of anything else you have heard (seen, etc.)?" "How does it make you feel?" "Do you have some idea why you hear these voices; why do they say what they do?"

At this point, the therapist may have already begun to form some idea about the dynamic meaning of the hallucination. He should determine the extent to which the patient is convinced that the hallucination is a perception of something real in the external world. He can ask the patient: "Do you see it?" "Might this be the work of your imagination?" "Could we explain this in some other way?" Finally, the therapist may be able to make an upward interpretation of the hallucination.

To a patient who repeatedly heard hostile voices addressing scatological words to him, the therapist remarked, "It occurs to me that those are the kinds of thoughts you sometimes have about yourself." To a patient who had persecutory delusions and heard identifiable voices saying "I'll get you yet," the therapist suggested, "Perhaps you yourself have some angry feelings toward those people."

Such "interpretations," actually clarifications, usually deal with the projective nature of delusions and hallucinations and do not magically cause the delusional thoughts to disappear overnight. However, they tacitly foster a way of working in therapy in which the patient and therapist agree that they can look at, and talk about, everything. Thoughts and feelings, no matter how unusual, are potentially understandable.

These principles, of course, are the basis for therapy with all patients, regardless of diagnostic category, and in all forms of psychotherapy. The principal issue here is the *level* of understanding which the therapist believes is appropriate. For patients who can tolerate brief regressions and moderate anxiety, clarifications relating to preconscious matters can be made. Further down the spectrum, the psychotic patient needs no further regression, nor should he be burdened with new causes for anxiety. He may be able, however, to look at some of the more obvious reasons for his thoughts and feelings.

INTERACTING WITH THE PATIENT

The more a patient is regressed and out of touch with reality, the more it behooves the therapist not to be an anonymous, shadowy person, but a very well delineated individual willing to interact with his patient. A psychotic patient, especially in an acute stage, may have difficulty knowing where his body and mind end and where those of another person begin—what is described as a loss or blurring of "ego boundaries." The therapist should attempt specifically to distinguish himself from the patient. To a very regressed schizophrenic youth, not yet responding to neuroleptic medication, a therapist might repeatedly say things like: "Hello John, how are you?" "Do you remember me? I am Doctor Smith," "Is that your hair brush?" "This is my pipe," etc.

In this regard, it is important with all patients, but much more so with severely regressed individuals, never to assume anything from unclear statements they make. One should tactfully ask for clarification and amplification: "Tell me a little more about that," or "I don't think I really understood what you said. Please tell it to me again" (or "differently" or "in some other way"). Therapists are sometimes uneasy about asking patients about delusions, hallucinations, and suicidal and homicidal thoughts because of a concern that talking about such thoughts will keep them in awareness or even lead the patient to act on them. Although it is unwise to try and go beyond what is clearly in awareness, there is no need to avoid what is already there. One is not likely to "put such thoughts in the patient's head" if they are not already there.

ALLIANCE WITH REALITY

The therapist must never permit himself the luxury of wandering from reality—as many of us do privately in dreams and fantasy. He must consistently ally himself with reality—in support of the ego—at all times. This does not mean that each and every time the patient distorts reality he must be challenged; were he to do this, the therapist would soon be experienced as a nag, or, worse, as a persecutor. However, the concept of the "red thread"—the dynamic direction of the patient's comments during a given hour—applies to supportive as well as to insight-oriented psychotherapy, and the therapist should deal with those misperceptions that are most related to the "red thread." This can be done tactfully by comments such as: "Are you sure?" "Really?" "Did you actually see (or hear) that?" "Could some *feelings* you had about that have influenced your ideas about it?," etc. The corollary of these tactful confrontations is the acknowledgment of good reality testing: at times the therapist should validate the patient's perceptions by telling him, "Yes, that's about the way I see it also," or "It must have been difficult for you to admit that (things are that way) (about yourself)."

Denial, projection, and splitting are the ego defenses which flout reality most severely. Their frequent use by an individual leads to severe problems in adaptation, object relationships, and interpersonal relations. Although every human being occasionally employs these primitive means of denying an unpleasant reality within himself or in his environment, the critical issue is the extent to which these defenses are used. To the extent that they are prominent in a person's psychological life, they remove him from close, effective contact with reality. Ultimately, they may result in a delusional reshaping of reality and a psychosis. It is for that reason that it is a fundamental task for the therapist to deal with these defenses.

No one enjoys being told—no matter how tactfully—that his grasp of reality is faulty. Consequently, when a therapist confronts such distortions, his motivation can easily be misconstrued and provoke an argumentative struggle. Moreover, the patient may deal with the confrontation itself by means of the same defenses—denial, projection or splitting—to deny the challenge. I should emphasize that these are not the only defenses used by patients in supportive psychotherapy; any and every defense may be used.

Barbara O., a 32-year-old housewife, had severe problems arising from low self-esteem associated with ego deficits. In therapy, this led her to frequently accuse her therapist that he did not like her, that he didn't think much of her, that he actually hated her and wished to get rid of her as a patient. On a day following a snowstorm, she was late for her appointment. While waiting for her, the therapist had begun reading a journal. He suddenly became aware that she had been standing, for perhaps a minute, in his doorway. He put down the journal and asked her to come in. She remained silent for several minutes, breathing somewhat rapidly, her face suffused with anger as she twisted her fingers around each other. After a while the therapist remarked that she seemed to be having some strong feelings, a comment which she ignored. After another few minutes, he said that she "seemed very tense." She burst into a tirade of accusations, claiming that she was sure he had not wanted her to come for her appointment, that he must have hoped she would be unable to drive through the snow so that he would be able to enjoy the free hour reading his "dumb psychiatric magazine." Without any leads from the patient, he hypothesized that she was angry with him for some previous slight she believed she had experienced from him, but that her rage had been unacceptable to her and could not be acknowledged to him or even to herself. He further speculated that although she was angry with him, she also felt she needed him and feared that if she were to tell him of her anger he would send her away.

With these conjectures in mind, he told her that it occurred to him that she was angry with him perhaps because at their last meeting he had told her he was unable (due to scheduling problems) to change her hours, as she had requested. Mrs. O. was pensive for a moment and then replied she always "knew" he didn't "give a damn" about her—he was "just doing a job." The therapist said, "Sometimes when you have strong angry feelings about *me*, you tend to feel that I must feel that way about *you*. It gives you another reason to be mad at me."

Needless to say, Mrs. O.'s reliance on projection did not disappear at the moment of the foregoing clarification, which was one of numerous discussions of her use of projection. Over a two-year period, Mrs. O. gradually recognized that she used projection very pervasively and also discovered that the therapist did not throw her out of his office if she berated him, nor did he retaliate in any other way. He consistently took the position that Mrs. O. injured herself by imputing to others her own unacceptable feelings. She began to think about what her feelings might have been when she felt others were having negative feelings about her. At the same time that she began to sense that there was really nothing "wrong" in having, for example, hostile feelings toward someone, she began to feel uncomfortable when she found herself attributing what she realized were her own feelings to someone else. She began to examine whether she "really" was angry with the person and why. Mrs. O. continued to use projection over a long period of time, but she did so less frequently, became less tenacious in insisting on the other person's malevolence towards her, and occasionally she even showed flashes of understanding how and why she used projection.

TRUST AND PARANOIA

Projection, like most human behavior, has gradations from mild and transitory to severe and chronic. It can result in pervasive but more or less reasonable suspiciousness on the one hand, to frank paranoia at the other extreme. On the same spectrum lies trust, without which any form of psychotherapy falters and often fails. Severe problems in trust seem related to experiences very early in life and can be exacerbated by cultural experiences and stereotypic group fantasies. Some therapists attempt to force trust from patients who have no reason to trust them. It is useful for the therapist to acknowledge an absence of trust, perhaps by simply saying he hopes the patient will, in time, be able to find him trustworthy.

In the meantime, the therapist continues to present himself as a nonjudgmental, concerned, listening helper, who offers to assist the patient in whatever reasonable way the patient requests. There is little point, for example, in challenging a patient's delusions until he has accepted the therapist as an ally. The development of a therapeutic relationship—the acceptance by the patient of the therapist as a trustworthy helper—is the basis for psychotherapeutic work with any patient and should be the therapist's primary concern during the first phase of treatment. It is clearly difficult to establish rapport with a delusional, or even suspicious patient, but the attempt must be made since little can be gained without it and the gains are potentially great. If the patient can learn to trust one person to a significant extent, there may be a genuine possibility of extending that trust to include other people.

The deeply suspicious or paranoid patient will forever be on the alert for a chink in the therapist's armor; he will test and retest, surreptitiously provoke, and overtly attack until he can demonstrate to the therapist that he, the patient, was right all along in his belief that the therapist *cannot* be trusted. Furthermore, the patient feels that he is in control of the relationship. When a therapeutic relationship has begun to develop, the therapist can tentatively begin to demonstrate how the patient's behavior sometimes engenders hostile reactions in the people around him. The severely maladaptive effect of his paranoid ideas should repeatedly be pointed out because, even if the patient is not prepared to give up a delusion, he may see the utility of not acting on it as though it were real.

As noted earlier, the patient's misperceptions can be confronted tactfully and piecemeal. The connection between his paranoia and his feelings of vulnerability, humiliation, and being out of control can be explained to him in order to help him understand that there are reasons why he feels and thinks the way he does. The paranoid patient may never say or indicate that he has begun to trust his therapist; but if he persists in coming for therapy, and if he continues to share even some of his thoughts and feelings with the therapist, then one can assume that some rapport has been established. That rapport should be carefully nurtured since it may be the only support the patient possesses. If the positive connection is disrupted, the therapist should set about trying to reestablish it; it should become his principal goal. With paranoid patients, the therapist should be particularly aboveboard, consistent, and candid. Any overt mistake he makes, or anything he says or does that the patient has apparently seen and that may hurt the therapeutic relationship, should be acknowledged. If it is appropriate to do so, apologies should be given to the patient.

Mrs. O. used splitting extensively in her relations with people. Because of her use of splitting as well as projection, it is not surprising that she was a very isolated, embittered, and embattled woman. Again, as with projection, the best arena for dealing with splitting is in the context of the therapeutic relationship. It is often very difficult to accurately assess a complicated situation reported by a patient who has tended to distort. Even if the therapist has a good idea of what happened, he is at a disadvantage because the patient can easily challenge him. Since the therapist was not present when the incident occurred, the patient feels that he has "no right" to comment on it. Mrs. O.'s feelings towards her therapist were extremely volatile, ranging from pure idealization to total deprecation. She could change her attitude toward him in a matter of minutes, depending on her interpretation of what he said or did—or did not say or do. Her exquisite vulnerability to humiliation, her fragile self-esteem, was typically the pivot on which her feelings turned and which led to her poor testing of reality.

After a year and a half of weekly sessions, in a therapy hour in which Mrs. O. was relaxed and friendly, she described a conflict she was having with her 12-year-old daughter. She had discovered that her daughter had lied to her about some household chore she was to have carried out. Although the girl denied lying, Mrs. O. had gone ahead and punished her quite severely—"grounding" her for a month. The therapist considered the punishment to be excessive and tactfully, he thought, wondered if a milder penance would not have been appropriate. In addition (it is usually not advisable to make more than one point at a time), he wondered whether it would have perhaps been more useful for Mrs. O. to try and understand *why* her daughter had been unable to tell her the truth. Although he said he "wondered" and used the word "perhaps," such qualifications were lost on the patient who accused him of "always taking my daughter's side against me," and "thinking I'm unfit to be a mother."

She went on to remind him of other alleged "insults" she had "continually" had to endure from him since their first meeting. The therapist was chagrined, having believed that he had established a reasonably solid rapport with Mrs. O. Had he felt more impelled to defend the value of his statements to the patient, the hour might quickly have degenerated into a debate on "Who is right?" Instead, feeling Mrs. O.'s humiliation at her thought that he found her to be an inadequate mother, he simply told her, "You must be very upset to think that I don't believe you are a good mother. That's hard to accept." The patient heard herself being listened to (or "followed," or "tracked"), and much of her rancor subsided.

A little later in the same hour, the therapist was able to show her how she had impulsively "cast him into darkness," despite the good work they had done together. More in control, Mrs. O.

said, "Yes, I haven't forgotten that, but you were insulting." The therapist said that he hadn't meant to be insulting but perhaps he had been. Then he added: "Even if I said something that upset you, even if I did something that wasn't right, it only means that like everyone else I'm not perfect and that I make mistakes. I'm truly sorry that we didn't understand each other, but I think we can still work together."

In this way, the therapist attempted to maintain his empathic posture; avoid repeating some of the patient's earlier experiences in which her family did not permit her to disagree with them; counsel her in a nonjudgmental manner; and, perhaps above all, demonstrate to her how she tended to distort what people thought of her because of her difficulty in accepting them as human beings who inevitably are less than perfect.

11

Typical Situations and Techniques:
Independence

A fundamental characteristic of a mature individual is the ability to be independent. This concept has never been satisfactorily defined but seems to encompass the idea that an individual is able to realize his maximum potential for doing and working; is able, within the limits of his possibilities, to utilize his own strengths in the day-to-day issues which confront him; and is able to deal with the major issues in life—career, values, sexual behavior, marriage and reproduction, object loss, personal sickness, aging and death.

Independence does not imply an inability to depend on others when that is necessary—as in sickness. Indeed, it is the pseudoindependent person who is unable to lean on others when necessary. The world is a highly integrated system, and it is impossible to live in total independence of others; we are connected to the people around us by innumerable ties of varying importance. Thus, to be independent means not only to be aware of one's own strength but of one's interdependence with others.

INDIVIDUATION

Independence is really another way of describing the situation of the individual whose ego functions generally operate at a reasonably optimal level. Most profoundly, it relates to the individual's conscious and, especially, unconscious conviction that he is truly a separate and unique individual. This, in turn, is the result of favorable circumstances surrounding the early development of his sense of self as distinct from the mother. The child normally delights in being on his own, develops a sense of what he can and cannot accomplish, tries to do what he feels capable of, and calls for help in situations that he actually cannot handle by himself. In typical circumstances he feels neither omnipotent nor impotent.

Beyond this fundamental process of individuation, the child acquires mastery of his biological endowments—motor behavior, perception, memory, and consciousness. Unless conflictual processes interfere, these endowments develop relatively smoothly. Other ego functions evolve which lead to further independence: reality testing, focused thinking, the ability to gratify drives in appropriate ways, the ability to have attachments to others which neither engulf nor destroy the one or the other, and the harmonizing of all these functions into a relatively conflict-free personality.

DEPENDENCE ON OTHERS

Many of the patients seen in supportive psychotherapy have significant difficulties in regard to independence, of which the most common relates to their excessive, ongoing need to lean on other people. These patients carry within them feelings of helplessness which are not unlike those experienced by depressed individuals. Their needs from other people are various: love, food (directly or symbolically), emotional support, advice and guidance, restraint of impulses and permission to gratify them without guilt.

Many such patients are prone to defend against their desire to be dependent by an exaggerated independence. Others desire independence but are afraid of it and cling with hostility to their therapist. They want a closer relationship with the therapist, but the closer they get, the more they feel dependent and the more they want to flee from a contact which they feel threatens the little independence they possess.

There is no simple solution in working with these patients, and their management has to be considered in the context of all the individual patient's ego functions, those which are deficient as well as those which are adequate. The encouragement of independence in patients who are deficient in it should infuse all therapeutic work.

Charles B., a 40-year-old unmarried bookkeeper, had a lifelong history of social isolation. He had always lived with his mother who suffered from cardiovascular disease and disabling arthritis. Mr. B. held a low-level position in a small firm, where he worked by himself in a tiny room; he received a salary which was clearly substandard. His employer had complete confidence in him and was pleased to have such a competent worker, especially one who only once in almost 20 years had asked for a raise in salary. Since Mr. B. lived rent-free in his mother's house and she paid for their utilities and food, his small salary was adequate for his needs which were, in any event, extraordinarily meager.

Mr. B. came for help, encouraged, if not actually brought, by his employer who had become concerned about Mr. B.'s recent marked loss of interest in his work. His mother had had a severe myocardial infarction four months earlier, and her possibly imminent death seemed to have shaken Mr. B.'s world. As the result of an evaluation, he was diagnosed as a "schizoidal personality" with poor object relations, infrequent impulsive episodes of homosexual activity, rather marked and almost paranoidal fantasies of persecution, and sublimatory activities virtually limited to nightly television watching. He grumbled about the ways in which his employer took advantage of him, the emptiness of his existence, and the futility of life in general. He dreaded to think about his mother dying since it would leave him bereft of any human relationship. He fantasied that if he were alone, he would have no place to live and would become a street person—hungry, cold, and uncared for.

From the outset of therapy, Mr. B. began making coy demands of the therapist for various small favors such as changing appointments, opening a window, etc. When the therapist suggested that the requests might be the patient's way of expressing his concern about whether the therapist would support him as his mother had done, he grew sullen and retreated into silence.

He was highly resistant to any suggestions the therapist made that might help him be more independent of his mother. In fact, the more the therapist tried to foster even modest steps toward autonomy, the more did Mr. B. cling to his dependent position.

At one point, when it appeared that the patient might be preparing to stop therapy, the therapist shifted his tactics and focused on Mr. B.'s long-smoldering rage at his mother. The first few times he broached this issue, he was strongly rebuffed. He then began to make the observation to the patient that it seemed Mr. B.'s mother was actually dependent on him rather than the opposite; and he wondered whether the patient might not have some feelings about how she was exploiting her illness to bind him to her even more strongly than she had in the past. This eventually led the patient to reveal a series of sadistic fantasies he had been having about his mother, and he described his life-long fear that if he ever "told her off" she would throw him out of the house and he would perish. The patient admitted that he had been terrified to tell the therapist about the terrible thoughts and feelings he had towards his mother. He also acknowledged that he had experienced the same kind of hostile and dependent feelings towards the therapist and said he had been surprised, on several occasions when he had balked at the therapist's suggestions, that he had not summarily been thrown out of treatment.

From approximately this time in therapy, he began to explore in some detail just how he might deal with his mother, how much time he could take for himself, what his real obligations to her were, and how he might cope with her temper tantrums and other ways she manipulated him. The patient mentioned that many years before he had enjoyed singing in a civic choral group, and was rather proud of his tenor voice. The therapist casually asked him if he thought his voice was still in form. Not long after, Mr. B. joined a similar group which enabled him to get away from the house one or two evenings a week. Although he did not develop any close relationships with other people in the chorus, he felt gratified simply by being with them and accepted by them, and he felt a little better about himself. Over the next few years, the therapist saw the patient less and less frequently. Some two years later, when Mr. B.'s mother died, he came for a visit to talk about it with his therapist; although anxious about the future, he seemed to be handling the mourning process adequately.

should use every opportunity to support and expand this quality in his patients. A good model for this can be seen in families in which the parents encourage independence to the extent that their child can handle it. Independence cannot be pushed or retarded excessively without ill effects. The parent who sees that the child is ready for more autonomy permits and encourages appropriate behavior. Even if the result is less than ideal, the experience of learning and tolerating some disappointment is invaluable. The child who has been encouraged to do something which ends poorly may well have been the victim of mistaken parental judgment, but it is usually not disastrous; the child can be reassured and deterred from going ahead for a while until there are good reasons to expect that he will succeed at the given task the next time.

In the same way, the therapist should permit the patient to do the work and make his own decisions whenever possible. When the patient asks for his opinion, the therapist should ask the patient, "What might you do?" Useful statements about a perplexing situation include: "What do you make of it?" "Perhaps something you are feeling is making it difficult for you to understand the situation," "Let's look at it."

Donald J., a brilliant undergraduate student, suffered from manic-depressive illness and had significant problems concerning dependency; he was obliged to take a leave of absence from college for at least one year, during which time he was advised to undergo psychotherapy in order to be eligible to rematriculate. After several months of treatment, although his therapist was unsure whether Mr. J. would be able to tolerate being in a classroom for a full hour, he decided to support his patient's request that he might return to school after having been on leave for only one semester.

His misgivings proved to be correct; after three weeks of erratic attendance in classes and inadequate preparation, Mr. J. was again obliged to ask for a withdrawal on medical grounds. He felt humiliated, but especially ashamed toward his therapist whom he felt he had "let down." He believed that his college career had come to an ignominious end and that he would have to give up his wish for a career in science.

The therapist told Mr. J. that he could understand his bitter

The principal issue here is the therapist's focus on Mr. B
developing some degree of independence. The major obstacle
the patient's becoming more independent was his intense ra
with his mother, his feelings of total dependence on her, and H
fear that if he ever indicated to her how much he hated her, sl
would drive him away, with catastrophic results. Consequentl
when the therapist at first directly attempted to convince Mr.
to move away from his mother, he rebelled, experiencing this
the irrevocable loss of his anchor. However, when the therap
was able to let him express his rage at his mother, and later
the therapist, the patient began to see that the earth did n
tremble. At least to a modest extent he became better able to lo
at ways of freeing himself from his mother.

AVOIDING THE DOGMATIC

Although the therapist had been on the wrong track at fir
his empathic "following" of the patient brought him closer
more effective work. Frequently, a therapist can find the m
useful path only by trial and error. It is for that reason that
should almost always avoid being adamant, dogmatic, and p
emptory, not only in what he says to a patient, but in his thinkin
Psychological reality is too intricate for any individual always
be "sure" of "all the truth." James Thurber's moral—it is bet
to know some of the questions than all of the answers—is a use
caution. Qualified statements, suggestions, opinions—identifi
as such—are generally the most acceptable ways of present
ideas to a patient.

It may be reassuring and gratifying to a therapist's narcissi
to be directive, authoritative, and parental, but if he is aware
the patient's struggle for independence—of thought, feelings, a
action—he will try to limit these countertherapeutic trends in h
self as he struggles to foster his patient's growth. Needless
add, such efforts by the therapist cannot help but foster his o
personal growth and professional development.

PROMOTING INDEPENDENCE

Independence is so crucial to most people's self-esteem an
the harmony they attain in living in the world, that the thera

disappointment, but that both he and the patient had miscalculated Mr. J.'s readiness to return to school, and he suggested that they try to understand where they had gone wrong. Mr. J. reluctantly agreed, and he and the therapist were able to make some headway in understanding why they had misjudged the situation. This generally had to do with wishful fantasies which caused them both to overvalue small indications of equilibrium in Mr. J. Although Mr. J. seemed ready to begin the next semester, he himself decided to wait six more months. At that later time, he reenrolled and, despite a very shaky beginning, was able to finish the semester with a reasonably good record.

In Mr. J.'s treatment, the therapist kept the issue of independence at the center of his therapeutic field. In every discussion about what Mr. J. was to do, he repeatedly emphasized the patient's role in making decisions and in carrying them out. When he and the patient disagreed about the premature return to college, he chose to permit him to take a reasonable chance of succeeding in the belief and hope that he could learn more from trying and not succeeding than from having been directed to stay out an additional semester.

Throughout his year of therapy, Mr. J. frequently raised the issue of moving back home, stating that he could see a therapist in his home city, that it would save money, that he wasn't attending school anyway, etc. Although all of this was undoubtedly true, as the therapist readily admitted, he also pointed out that once the patient was back home his parents would again begin to treat him like a child, a situation to which he was only too susceptible.

Another aspect of supporting Mr. J.'s autonomy concerned the lithium carbonate which the therapist had prescribed. Before prescribing lithium, the therapist gave a careful explanation of the value to Mr. J. of this medication for control of his manic-depressive illness. The patient alternated between wanting to refuse medication as a "chemical straitjacket" and wanting to receive it as a form of parentally sanctioned regression. Both aspects of the problem were discussed until the therapist felt that the patient was much more in agreement to take the medication than not to do so. It would have been of little or no avail for the patient to be forced to fill his prescription only to take the lithium erratically or not at all.

After several weeks into his next semester, Mr. J. announced that he felt he no longer needed to see his therapist. Again the matter was discussed at length, and after several weeks an agreement was reached that his visits of once a week would be reduced to once every two weeks and finally to half an hour once a month. Mr. J. continued to take his medication regularly (as periodic laboratory determinations showed). Also, he was conscientious and sensitive enough to realize when he was getting into difficulty and would then call for an additional appointment.

Flexibility, empathy, and focus were the key factors that made this treatment successful. Mr. J. will probably continue to take lithium indefinitely, but it is likely that he will take it of his own accord and, therefore, with some regularity. His marked disinclination for introspection and his general contentment with his psychological makeup, if not his episodes of depression and mania, suggest that his level of independence will be limited. Nevertheless, it had expanded modestly during the course of supportive psychotherapy. His profound yearning to be dependent will remain his vulnerable trait and will leave the door ajar for subsequent disappointments and episodes of depression.

TOLERATING PAINFUL FEELINGS

One is struck by the difficulty experienced by many of the patients seen in supportive psychotherapy to tolerate painful feelings. Such intolerance, when pronounced, may be a major determinant in not initially recommending insight-oriented treatment for some people since such therapy is always more or less traumatic, while supportive treatment, by definition, is structured not to be traumatic—or at least no more so than is clearly tolerable for the patient.

Frequently, like a suffering child, a patient in supportive psychotherapy has the feeling that his psychological pain will go on indefinitely; he seems unable to grasp the fact that anxiety, depression, etc., especially when situational, are usually self-limited. Consequently, the therapist must help the patient realize that the pain will disappear. He should be careful not to make predictions, which may well be unreliable, but rather to point out that the patient himself can try to change his condition. The patient may be adamant in refusing to engage in behavior that will modulate, even temporarily, what he is feeling. Still, such "diversions" may be very helpful. Despite the patient's resistance ("I've tried that and it won't work," "I can't keep it going," "It's useless," "It's easy for you to say," etc.), the therapist should continue to encourage the patient to "keep going," to keep putting one foot in front of the other, whether that means staying on his job, engaging in leisure activities, etc.

Perhaps the most valuable aspect of the therapist's work is to get across to the patient that he has understood what the patient is going through. Pain of all sorts seems more tolerable if someone else is aware of what we are feeling. Unless this empathic response to the patient exists, any suggestions or comments the therapist makes will be sterile and of limited value. When an observing ego is deficient, the development of positive rapport and the therapist's empathy are critical factors in maintaining the therapeutic process.

Individuals who have reached adulthood with a particular intolerance for even moderate levels of mental suffering arrive at this stage via many paths. Usually, however, their childhood was marked, as is the case in so many emotional disturbances, either by excessive, painful frustration or by massive overindulgence. To attempt to modify this intolerance of psychological pain is very difficult, and little has been specifically written about it. I believe that perhaps the most useful instrument is the therapist's empathic attitude, as the following vignette illustrates.

Arthur K. was the newest junior executive with his firm. He was authoritarian with his young secretary who was unable to defend herself against his excessive demands. However, another secretary, a mature woman, long with the firm, who often did some work for Mr. K., took it upon herself to champion her associate. Since she was quite clever in repartee, Mr. K. often felt that he came off second best. On the morning of the therapy hour in question, Mr. K. discovered that this woman, Mrs. Howard, had sent off a letter to an important client of the firm with an inappropriate salutation and closing. Mr. K. was understandably angry, but she insisted that that was the way he had dictated it; the tape had been reused, and the argument quickly degenerated into thinly veiled personal attacks.

Finally, Mr. K. accused Mrs. Howard of deliberately making the mistake. When she responded (not altogether incorrectly) that he was being "paranoid," he went to a company officer and demanded that Mrs. Howard be fired immediately. The officer refused to fire a highly competent and trusted employee, almost implied that she was more valuable to the firm than was Mr. K., and suggested that Mr. K. "work it out" with her. In therapy, Mr. K.'s rage was monumental; he pounded the arms of his chair, shouted, declared he couldn't "stand any more of this," and vowed that he was going to "kick the shit out of that rotten bitch."

That he was suffering from an intense narcissistic humiliation was evident; it was clear that he had been projecting his hostility (for which there was, at least, the traditional "kernel" of truth) onto Mrs. Howard. He appeared to be nearly out of control. His therapist chose to deal with the projection of Mr. K.'s hostility onto Mrs. Howard and suggested that that was why he suspected her of sabotaging his efforts. The therapist quickly realized his tactical mistake as Mr. K. diverted his anger from Mrs. Howard towards him.

Recovering his empathy, the therapist remarked, "It must have been very humiliating to feel you were treated as expendable and less important to the firm than a secretary, especially since you have been trying to demonstrate your ability by hard work and innovative ideas." Mr. K. burst into tears. When he resumed talking, he began to connect the incident with the company officer to other situations in his life in which he had not been appreciated—particularly on the many occasions when his highly successful father had criticized his faults, but rarely said anything positive about him. Later, he was able to look at and recognize his use of projection in the battle with Mrs. Howard. What seemed to help him to tolerate his humiliation was his sense that his feelings were understood by the therapist, who without telling Mr. K. that his feelings were justified, empathically allied himself with the patient in his suffering.

Mourning rituals, from time immemorial, attest to the soothing effect other people can have on the individual who is grief-stricken. Empathic support does not in itself lead the patient to be able to endure anxiety, depression, or other painful feelings, but it makes a start by providing an external source of soothing, much as a mother does for a small child. Over a period of time, the patient feels less desperate about his anguish, having seen that with the therapist he is more able to "ride it out." Such experiences, especially when the therapist points them out to the patient, permit him to be more accepting of his pain. Under appropriate circumstances the therapist can observe that the patient really is capable of tolerating suffering. His own patient, empathic, and understanding attitude will tend, to some degree, to be internalized and adopted by the patient who may gradually be able to say to himself: "I've managed to get through this before, I shall do so again."

Every small achievement the patient makes should be noted by the therapist in a frankly rewarding way in which the reward is the approval of someone whom the patient esteems. In effect, what the therapist is doing is supplying the kinds of experiences the patient lacked as a child in the hope, if not the expectation, that he will be able to internalize the therapist's attitude towards emotional pain. Even if the patient is unable to develop a greater tolerance for his pain, he will suffer less because of the therapist's kind support—and that, in itself, is an important function of a therapist: to alleviate suffering.

12

Typical Situations and Techniques:
Impulsive Behavior and Passivity

A patient's behavior, in the sense of denoting his actions, toward himself or others may of necessity be the first issue that the therapist must deal with in supportive psychotherapy when the behavior is about to become a critical matter—if it has not already become so.

Unthinking, impulsive behavior can be conceptualized broadly as either characterological or neurotic. Characterologically rooted behavior is pervasive and generally lifelong, having its basis in significant deviations in the child's early development when he ordinarily learns to delay gratification and to think before he acts. It may also be influenced by constitutional factors—a relationship which is poorly understood. Neurotically rooted behavior derives more from specific, underlying *conflicts* with which the individual is trying to deal through his actions; it typically represents a compromise between a forbidden impulse and the defense against that impulse.

CHARACTEROLOGICAL IMPULSE DISORDERS

A characterological impulse disorder suggests that the patient has never developed the necessary ego functions to deal with impulses—chiefly hostile ones, but also to some extent, sexual impulses. The individual continues to experience the need for immediate release of his feelings through behavior which may range from childlike temper tantrums to highly destructive anti-social behavior. It is said that males tend to lose control of their hostile impulses more readily than females, whereas the latter may have greater difficulties controlling "sexual" impulses. Such ideas may contain some truth but should be taken with a grain of salt since the nature of the impulse in question is often unclear.

For the therapist who is dealing with impulse-ridden patients, the therapeutic problem is extremely difficult, not only because these patients have a long history of acting before thinking, but because the act in itself (as is a neurotic act) is pleasurable by virtue of its being a derivative way of gratifying aggressive and/or sexual urges. The more such behavior fulfills those needs, that is, the more pleasurable it is to the individual, the more entrenched it is in the entire fabric of his life.

Perhaps the most effective means of treating these patients is through identification: the therapist becomes, to some extent, a model for the patient. This may relate to several features of the therapist's behavior but, insofar as it concerns impulses, the patient can see that his therapist thinks before he acts: He examines a plan of action with the patient and tries to enlist the patient's commitment to delaying gratification. The therapist constantly supports the notion of thought as a form of trial action. He does not denigrate drive impulses as such, nor action, nor gratification; what he does point out is the self-protective necessity to "think first," that this is always in the interest of the patient and those whom the patient loves.

PROMOTING ALTERNATIVE BEHAVIORS

When certain kinds of behavior are simply not possible because they cause the patient intolerable guilt or are illegal or dangerous, the therapist should try to guide the patient into safer, more ego-syntonic channels for discharging his impulses. Such alternative activities not only can satisfy the impulse but also make the patient's life richer and less chaotic. The search for sublimatory activities appropriate for a given patient often requires much ingenuity and imagination. The therapist should attempt to encourage any constructive interest the patient possesses, no matter how slight or long unused.

Activities that are readily available to many patients such as gardening, fishing, spectator and participant sports, dancing, musical groups, walking, hiking, or camping trips, etc., are preferable to activities having requirements—special location, skill, need for a group, etc.—that often automatically provoke resistance in the patient. If the patient has, in the past, enjoyed some particular activity such as playing chess, sewing, cooking, doing an artistic or craft activity, etc., it is useful to foster it since the patient is already familiar and probably comfortable with it.

THE "PEDAGOGIC" APPROACH

Perhaps the most telling impact the therapist can make, to the extent that it is at all successful, is essentially pedagogic: he must tirelessly demonstrate that although impulsive behavior may "feel good" at the moment, there is ultimately a self-destructive aspect to it which usually more than negates the original pleasure. In counseling patients who have been involved in antisocial behavior, the therapist must be careful not to fall into the well-known trap of advising them how to keep out of trouble by not getting caught—in effect helping them to become more adept in their sociopathy. The history of rehabilitation of antisocial personalities is, unfortunately, lamentably unreassuring. Nevertheless, as with all patients, the task is to discover what is healthy in the patient's psychological makeup and to encourage and reward it. On the spectrum of ego strength, those patients who are the most mature will tend to be appropriate candidates for a psychotherapy that seeks to develop insight and will have the best prognosis. However, those with weak ego strength are candidates for supportive therapy, and the prognosis for this group is necessarily guarded or poor.

IMPULSIVE BEHAVIOR AND SUPPORTIVE PSYCHOTHERAPY

It is important not to use the nature of the patient's behavior itself as the guiding criterion for selection of patients for insight or supportive psychotherapy. Individuals with a record of criminal behavior, sex offenders, drug and alcohol abusers, etc., should be assigned to a particular form of psychotherapy on the basis of a total evaluation of their ego strengths, weaknesses, and all the characteristics of their superego. Some individuals who have been diagnosed as psychopathic may also be schizophrenic, belong to the borderline group, or have other significant characterological configurations. On the other hand, many patients who seem sociopathic may have acted out of neurotic conflicts—as in kleptomania or many sexual practices—and may be amenable to insight treatment.

The same cautionary note should be kept in mind especially when dealing with alcohol and drug abusers. Their substance abuse usually is what precipitates their entering treatment. However, it is but a derivative, important though it may be, of an underlying character problem. Whether the patient should enter supportive or insight-oriented psychotherapy will depend on the overall evaluation. In all situations related to behavior and impulse problems, the therapist should always decide whether the action represents a transitory, regressive phenomenon in an individual whose psychological development and psychological makeup are fundamentally normative, or whether the behavior is a lifelong expression of severe developmental and structural deficits.

By and large, patients whose impulsiveness is neurotic—that is, derives from unconscious conflict, defense, and adaptation—tend to be more suitable for insight-oriented psychotherapy than are those whose rash behavior is characterological. This is particularly true if the neurotic behavior has a relatively short history of occurrence, is especially alien to the patient, and can be seen as having been precipitated by specific events.

Nevertheless, such generalizations are no substitute for the careful evaluation of each patient. Indeed, regardless of the relative correctness of any generalization about a class of patients, whether it concerns culture, ethnic group, psychiatric diagnosis, social class, etc., each patient must be assessed according to his own specific characteristics. Thus, we find that many patients who are neurotically impulsive are not able to work in insight therapy. In fact, the patients who act neurotically constitute a heterogeneous group. Some of these individuals are characterized as having a hysterical personality and, therefore, are frequently

believed to be good candidates for insight-oriented psychotherapy. However, as Zetzel (1968) has shown, there are "good hysterics" and "so-called good hysterics." While some of the patients
included in the first group are indeed able to work in insight
treatment, most of the patients in the latter group should receive
supportive psychotherapy. What patients in the "so-called" group
actually demonstrate are one or more ego defects or deficiencies
which place them conceptually in the borderline group.

Clearly, "hysterical personality" refers to a group of patients
whose psychological makeup may be anywhere on a spectrum of
psychopathology, "structural problems" at one end and "conflict
problems" at the other end. Even so, one finds patients at the
conflict end of this spectrum who may be better treated in supportive psychotherapy because of other characteristics that have
been noted during the evaluation. For example, one often discovers that in addition to oedipal conflicts some of these patients
have significant problems relating to preoedipal fixations —typically concerning orality, independence, and a pervasive need for
nurturance.

Mrs. Edith G. had been married for 10 years and had two children. Her husband was the minister of a small congregation and
also held two part-time jobs in order to earn a modest income.
Mrs. G. had married hastily at age 16 because she was pregnant.
Before her marriage, she had had several brief love affairs with
boys her own age as well as with older men. Mr. G. was 15 years
older than his wife, and she became infatuated with him the first
time they met. The marriage seemed reasonably stable until the
second child entered school. Then Mrs. G. suddenly found herself
facing long days with little to do. Since her husband came home
for supper only to quickly leave again for work, her evenings
seemed empty, even though her children were at home. Mrs. G.
found her husband less and less "fun" and complained of "nothing to do." When he suggested various activities, she began to
regard him as downright irritating. Their frequent petty squabbles
led to sullen silences and less frequent sexual relations.

Mrs. G. became friendly with some women who shared a somewhat similar home life and progressively began to spend her evenings with them in various bars. She soon was having a variety
of affairs—mostly one-night stands. Mr. G. seemed oblivious to

what was happening until, coming home one night earlier than usual, he discovered her *in flagrante delicto* with a teenage boy from their neighborhood. After several stormy scenes, Mr. and Mrs. G. entered marital counseling, and Mrs. G. began once-a-week psychotherapy with another therapist.

Although the therapist at first believed that he could do insight work with this patient, it was soon apparent that that was not appropriate, and he shifted to supportive therapy. From the hours of individual therapy, the therapist learned that Mrs. G.'s husband had initially seemed attractive to Mrs. G. because she experienced him as her seductive father who had philandered to such an extent that Mrs. G.'s mother had thrown him out many years earlier. At the same time, Mrs. G. had intense desires to be mothered and held either by older men or by youths whom she could identify with and simultaneously control and mother.

In therapy, Mrs. G. wanted her wishes gratified "right now," and her attempts to seduce her therapist were overt, emotional, and theatrical. She had no interest or desire to explore the meaning of her behavior and bluntly told her therapist that she would continue to see him only as long as she might hope to have an affair with him. The therapist valiantly dealt with her seductive behavior towards him and finally was only able to approach the problem by having her look at the probable consequences of her behavior: divorce, possible loss of her children, ostracism by the community, harsh criticism by her own family, drastically reduced standard of living, etc. The therapist thus served as an auxiliary ego—he *supported* her against flawed reality testing. The real consequences of her behavior seemed to be the only issues that the patient could be brought to consider; when she did so, she realized that she had been playing a dangerous game with her husband.

The therapist urged her to *think* about what she was going to do *before* acting, rather than suffer the consequences of her impulsive behavior. In each reported situation in which Mrs. G. complained of someone else's behavior towards her, the therapist urged her to examine *her* role, *her* responsibility, in the difficulties she was having. He was careful to acknowledge the part the other person played when that was appropriate, but he repeatedly confronted her with her contribution to the problem. He patiently (and sometimes impatiently) showed her how she closed her eyes to her part in the situations, and that her behavior ("after all, what else could I do?") was not an inevitable reaction to external pressures. He showed her how her behavior often provoked reactions from other people to which she then reacted as though she had had no part in provoking them.

When Mrs. G. dramatically and flamboyantly exaggerated situations or feelings, the therapist generally would say, "Yes, I can see why you feel that way, but I think you're using a baseball bat to kill a mosquito; I wonder if you don't tend to make things bigger when you think about them." In the same way, he attempted to deal with her seductiveness and idealization of him by suggesting, "Perhaps some of your feelings about me have to do with your satisfaction in our working together," and, "I think it's very important to you that I think well of you." Later, when her seductive efforts came to nothing and she grew angry and spiteful toward her therapist, he said, "It occurs to me that you feel I rejected and insulted you because I haven't returned your affection. Can you think of some reason why I did not do so, other than that I don't think well of you?" Therapists sometimes deal reactively with seductive patients such as Mrs. G. by becoming cold and distant as a way of protecting themselves; this usually only makes matters worse.

In the concurrent marital therapy sessions, Mr. G. was able to understand his wife's behavior somewhat better, and arranged to spend more time with her. He began to realize that she needed, and would probably always need, more attention from him and that if it were not forthcoming she would seek it from other men.

After several months of individual supportive therapy, Mrs. G. felt she was no longer "getting anything out of it," and shortly thereafter marital counseling was terminated at the request of the couple. Despite some improvement, the prognosis was guarded both for the marriage and for Mrs. G. In this situation, the therapist's technical options were limited, dealing as he was with the kind of patient described by Freud as one who is interested only in the "logic of soup, with dumplings for arguments" (Freud, 1915).

ACTING-OUT

Acting-out is a particular form of neurotic behavior. The term itself has had an unfortunate history, having strayed too far from its original meaning and becoming a pejorative expression applied to any activity which one considers inappropriate, immoral, or indecent. In its more technical sense, acting-out describes transference attitudes and feelings which are expressed by overt actions rather than through thoughts and speech. Although acting-out may apply to the behavior of an individual not in psychotherapy who is repeating, with people in his current life, attitudes originally formed from his relationships with individuals in his childhood, it most accurately relates to an individual who is in treatment.

In such a situation, the patient's transference reactions are not verbalized but are cast in actions such as absences, lateness, displacement of feelings about the therapist onto other people in the patient's life, etc. Thus, a patient who is angry with his therapist may take out his feelings on someone at home or at work—often using some trivial event to justify his behavior and "externalize" the problem.

In psychotherapy which is aimed at developing insight through verbalizing thoughts and feelings and exploring them, such action becomes a serious obstacle in the therapeutic process. Furthermore, since a discussion of the impulse occurs after the act, it has a lesser sense of urgency than when the wish is still intense. Once the act has taken place, much of the emotional energy of the impulse is gone and the patient may wish to forget it, especially if talking about it might make him feel guilty. It must be noted that acting-out and acting-in (see below) are not the sole province of patients—unfortunately therapists may engage in such behavior. When the therapist has done so, or is aware of a strong urge to do so, it is necessary for him to examine carefully his interaction with the patient in an attempt to understand what provoked those impulses in him.

Acting-out can and does occur frequently in supportive psychotherapy. In these situations, it is less an obstacle in the path of understanding than a threat to the therapeutic relationship as such. Moreover, as with all such activity, it perpetuates gravely maladaptive behavior in addition to being potentially destructive.

Allied with acting-out is acting-in—activity during the therapy hour. This can take such benign forms as the patient putting his feet up on the therapist's desk or, more dangerously, physically assaulting the therapist. Since rageful reactions are not infrequent among the group of patients seen in supportive psychotherapy, such behavior is not rare and should be dealt with promptly and firmly, with specific limits set as to what is to be tolerated in the hour.

Many patients who are described as having a "borderline personality" are prone to frequent and intense reactions of rage, provoked by what often seems to an observer to be a most trivial event. At times these episodes are of such force and intensity that even experienced therapists will feel seared by the heat of the patient's violence and abuse. Not only is the menace frightening, but the therapist may be afraid of his own impulse to respond with similar violence. Not unusually, he may deal with his own hatred by a reaction formation—being excessively "nice" to the patient. He may profoundly wish for the patient to simply disappear from the face of the earth—how this might happen is secondary to the desire for this abusive and perhaps frightening patient to vanish from his life. To the extent that the therapist's response is overt and is perceived by the patient, there is little point in the therapist denying his feelings.

One patient rose from his chair and stood over his therapist with clenched fists, threatening him and shouting abuse; the therapist became anxious and enraged. "Sit down," he commanded, "and shut up!" Gleefully, the patient accused him of having become angry. "Yes," replied the therapist, "I don't like being yelled at and abused. I do want you to tell me what you are feeling, but I can't allow you to threaten me. You have to try and put into words what is bothering you so that we can try and understand where these feelings are coming from." Such setting of limits is of critical importance when working with patients who do not have sufficient inner resources to set their own limits. In all such situations, care must be taken that such limit setting not be a veiled form of punishment.

ACTING-OUT AND TRANSFERENCE

Since acting-out generally indicates the presence of transference, its occurrence indicates that the therapist must deal not only with the behavior but with the underlying transference. This can be done in two steps: the first is to develop in the patient an understanding that the behavior frequently represents current feelings about the therapist. The patient who begins to argue with a colleague at work may be expressing his irritation with his therapist. The second step is for the therapist to attempt to interpret the transference reaction itself through an upward interpretation. Thus, when Mrs. O. was angry with her therapist because he could not change her schedule, she may have been experiencing him as if he were her aloof and passively rejecting father. However, it would have sufficed for the therapist to inquire, "Could it be that you became angry with me because you felt I was rejecting you by not giving you the hours you wanted?"

ADAPTIVE DEFENSES AGAINST ACTING-OUT

In the same way that the therapist encourages the patient to put his feelings and thoughts into words rather than actions, so he also urges the patient to substitute less maladaptive defenses for more harmful ones. Although all defenses are ways of denying some painful reality, some, such as projection, make for gross distortions of reality—in contrast for example, to reaction formation, intellectualization and rationalization, which are rarely, if ever, destructive.

Sublimation, of course, is the most adaptive means of channeling sexual and aggressive impulses; some authors claim that it is not an ego defense in the same sense as the others mentioned; nevertheless, it can be a highly gratifying and effective means of coping with inner and outer stress and should always be encouraged. The following vignette illustrates how one piece of defensive behavior can be substituted for another more maladaptive behavior.

Florence U., a 23-year-old dietician, began to have the intrusive thought: "I am going to kill my child." At the first interview her reality testing seemed erratic, she was markedly dependent, used splitting and denial extensively and apparently possessed little or no psychological-mindedness. A cautious attempt to explore what had precipitated her symptoms was futile. Mrs. U. simply cried and declared she would "go crazy if these thoughts don't stop."

Her anguish was sufficiently intense for the therapist to place her on a minor tranquilizer, and suggested that every time the intrusive thought came into her mind she should go through a counting ritual (counting by two's to a hundred; if the thought persisted or immediately returned, she was to count by two's from a hundred to zero). This ritual was offered as a substitute symptom for her much more painful intrusive thoughts. Not only did this technique displace one symptom by another, but implicit in the therapist's request that she do this was a suggestion, in the technical sense of the word, that by doing so Mrs. U. would obtain relief from the intrusive thoughts. At her next visit, three days later, Mrs. U. reported some diminution in her symptoms, and in three weeks they were almost gone. Subsequently, the patient was better able to begin to look at the events that had preceded her symptoms, and insight-oriented psychotherapy was gradually begun.

OBSESSIVE-COMPULSIVE INDIVIDUALS

In contrast to the impulse-ridden patients described earlier, there are those whose personalities are organized around the principle of avoiding any activity which might provoke mental suffering. Many of these patients are characterized as having an obsessive-compulsive character, or they may actually demonstrate classical obsessive-compulsive symptoms. These diagnoses, as with all the other psychological difficulties described, do not automatically indicate that a given patient should be treated with insight-oriented psychotherapy. One of the most difficult mental disturbances to treat—and which causes so much pain to the patient—is obsessive-compulsive illness; when leucotomies were more frequently performed for mental illness, it was high on the list of indications for such surgery.

Quite opposite from the typical hysterical patient, the life of the obsessive-compulsive individual is seemingly devoted to so much continual rumination that action becomes virtually impossible for him—which is precisely his unconscious goal: to avoid conflictual behavior that might lead to painful feelings of anxiety, guilt, shame or depression.

When patients with obsessive-compulsive character traits (parsimony, excessive cleanliness, stubbornness, etc.) or with obsessive-compulsive symptoms (intrusive thoughts, rituals, etc.) are seen in supportive psychotherapy, they may at times utilize these traits and symptoms to defend themselves against possibly severe regressions. If the clinical picture at the time of evaluation suggests that such regression is impending, the therapist should be careful not to diminish these essentially neurotic (as opposed to psychotic) defenses. In fact, if there are indications that the patient has begun to regress, as might be suggested by a loss of reality testing, primitive sexual behavior, loss of impulse control, or inability to continue working, the therapist should try to enhance existing obsessive-compulsive traits, or introduce new ones in an effort to ward off, slow down, or mitigate the regressive process. However, if regression does not seem to be an immediate problem, and the patient is suffering from his obsessive defenses and symptoms, he can frequently be helped to at least diminish the intensity of these painful traits. Unlike the patient whose neurotic symptoms barely manage to protect him from a psychotic breakdown, these patients are less precariously situated; they may be in some relative state of equilibrium, but their lives are bleak and crowded with compulsive behavior at the expense of more pleasurable activities.

George P. came to see a psychiatrist because his wife, he reported, had told him that unless he "changed his ways" she was likely to leave him. Mr. P. was a 38-year-old shop teacher in a junior high school. He had been married nine years and had two children. Although he initially claimed that his way of life did not bother him, it became clear that he was profoundly dissatisfied with himself. Since he had "always been like that," he had for many years felt hopeless about changing; in recent years he had simply "not thought much about it." He had once overheard one of his students refer to him as a "dried-up prune."

At home, his interaction with his wife and children was minimal; if Mrs. P. asked him to do something around the house, or to spend some time with the children, he would do so, but had little pleasure in doing things with them. One of his main problems was that the form of what he was doing had become more important than the content. In school he was intolerant of the way his students dressed and he judged their work by their personal neatness. In his woodworking shop at home, where he spent many pleasant, quiet hours, he often devoted more time to sweeping up, cleaning, rearranging and oiling his tools than to the project he was engaged in. Not surprisingly, he was extremely frugal and he literally counted his pennies.

In the course of his evaluation he wondered whether the doctor had a "special pill" that would "loosen" him up. When he was told that it would mainly be up to him to change, he was disappointed and asked the psychiatrist how he might go about changing. The therapist replied, "Perhaps if we could understand why you put yourself to such troubles we might find that much of it was unnecessary, and you might be able to give up some of this behavior you find so wearisome."

His therapist believed that Mr. P. was unable to benefit from insight-oriented psychotherapy, and he began simply to deal systematically with helping Mr. P. soften his rigid patterns of behavior. After about three months, it became clear that the patient was beginning to feel comfortable with his therapist. Each week he brought in an "agenda" of items he wanted to talk about. His inability to relax, to stop driving himself, seemed to be the result of a highly punitive conscience (superego) to which he had to constantly answer by being an exceptionally "good boy."

It was at first difficult to obtain a clear childhood history from Mr. P., but over time he began to allude to early punishments, apparently for masturbation. He described a father whom he experienced as harsh and unloving and a hypochondriacal mother who constantly told him that he would be "her death" because of his infractions of her "rules."

The therapist allied himself with the "pleasure principle" such as it existed in the patient. In effect, he began to cast doubt on the patient's "need" to be rigid. He rhetorically asked, "What does it serve?" When the patient asked him if he thought he ought to carry out an elaborate plan of atonement for a minor impoliteness with the principal of his school, the therapist said, "It strikes me that you've already apologized about enough. Do you think the principal wants you to crawl to him to ask forgiveness?" The patient ruefully responded that he didn't think so.

In every situation that Mr. P. brought up, the therapist attempted to deal with the patient's isolation of feelings. He consistently, in one way or another, pursued what the patient might be feeling. Mr. P. was especially ashamed of any but the most mild and banal emotions. When he was not invited to serve on a faculty committee, where he felt he could make a contribution, he was visibly hurt and angry, but insisted he "didn't care"—in fact, he said it would give him more free time. The therapist directly confronted him with his pressured speech, choked-up tone, etc., and said, "To me you look and sound like a man who felt he was slapped in the face." The patient was silent for a moment, and admitted that he had wanted to punch the principal in the face.

Whenever issues came up regarding some small pleasure or modest expense, Mr. P. wanted to know what his therapist thought he should do. The therapist usually responded in ways which generally gave the patient *permission* to go ahead, without specifically *telling* him what to do. He would say: "What harm could come from it?" "Would someone suffer from that?" "How difficult it is for you to enjoy things!"

Whenever possible, the therapist reminded the patient that earlier he had been able to do something similar to what he was now shying away from, or that he had once been able to decide on a path of action much like the one he was now avoiding. Although Mr. P. repeatedly wanted his doctor to tell him what to do (and when he did, would give him a dozen reasons why it was impossible), the therapist progressively encouraged Mr. P. to make decisions on his own. At first he suggested that they "work on this together" and he took the lion's share of the work. In time, he shifted his role to that of encouraging the patient, of applauding his good effort, and comforting him when he failed. Over the course of two years of supportive psychotherapy, these attempts were not without their effect, and when Mr. P. decided to stop treatment, both he and his therapist were gratified at the progress he had made.

Throughout the treatment, one of the principal contributions the therapist made was as an auxiliary superego. Instead of helping Mr. P. test reality—supporting an ego function—which he was able to do by himself, the therapist softened the patient's harsh and punitive conscience by giving him permission to enjoy life a little more than he had previously done and without fear of some awful retribution.

13

Typical Situations and Techniques:
The Silent Patient

The silent patient who is unable or unwilling to communicate verbally with his therapist exemplifies a situation that may be encountered in every form of psychotherapy and with patients suffering from a variety of psychological illnesses.

THE DEPRESSED PATIENT

One of the most difficult and painful situations occurs with severely depressed patients who can barely listen to what the therapist is saying to them; they are so profoundly enveloped in their misery and perplexity that the outside world often appears as a blur, while their own thought processes and attempts at communication feel so clumsy and woefully inadequate that they prefer to remain silent.

For such patients, except in special and unusual circumstances, the prescription of antidepressant medication is mandatory, and hospitalization usually indicated. Not only will pharmacological treatment relieve the patient's suffering, but after some weeks or sooner it may permit him to enter into a therapeutic relationship in which some form of psychotherapy can be carried out. In these situations, unless the therapist has had some previous contact with the patient, a decision regarding appropriateness for supportive or insight-oriented psychotherapy is bound to be somewhat speculative and tentative. If the patient is suicidal, unable to work, generally regressed and depressively retarded or agitated, or has not responded to antidepressant medication, hospitalization is definitely indicated.

Under more favorable circumstances, however, when the depression has subsided sufficiently so that some reasonable degree of contact between patient and therapist can be made, a more careful evaluation can be done. In such a situation, the same criteria that apply to any individual being evaluated for therapy will apply. Some of the patients for whom supportive psychotherapy is indicated will drop out of such treatment once their depression has lifted. Those who tend to remain in therapy are often patients with a history of previous episodes and those who have been suffering not from an acute depressive episode, but from what might aptly be called chronic depression. In fact, such a patient might well be described as having a depressive character. He has a more or less lifelong sense of the emptiness of his existence; moments of joy or even contentment are short-lived and infrequent. Even when there have been good times in his life, he has tended to dismiss them as unimportant and fleeting.

Some of these patients have what amounts to a suicidal character trait: their first thought when they become depressed is, "Well, I can always kill myself." Not infrequently, they have made suicidal threats, gestures, or attempts. The "trait" often first appeared at puberty or even earlier. Such a patient frequently is dependent, clinging, insatiable in his demands on the world around him for love and nurturance, in literal as well as symbolic forms. His insistent demands frequently lead him to be shunned by people which, in turn, makes him diffident about asking even for what is rightly his due. He then finds himself boxed into a position where if he asks for love, he tends to be rebuffed; if he withdraws, he feels lonely, empty, and rejected by everyone.

As a result, such patients possess a distorted view of the world as well as of themselves. They see the people around them as humiliating, cruel, and exploitative; and, more significantly, they experience themselves as unlovable, hateful, and incompetent.

Bibring on Depression

These psychodynamics were effectively worked out by Edward Bibring (1953) in his seminal paper on depression. He observed that a shock-like state develops in these patients when they experience a deep chasm between their strongly held "narcissistic aspirations"—their ideal self—and their view of themselves as falling painfully short of those aspirations. These ideals relate to being lovable, loving, and competent, and to not being hateful, hating, or incompetent.

These individuals, Bibring says, have become vulnerable to depressive episodes because of shocklike, traumatic experiences that occurred at any developmental level during their formative years. Depressive episodes in adult life tend to subside when the frustrated narcissistic goals again seem within reach; the patient lowers his sights to more realistically attainable goals; he entirely abandons the desired goals; he finds substitutes for them, or he defends himself against painful feelings of depression by experiencing a different feeling such as apathy, hypomania, or depersonalization.

STRATEGIES WITH DEPRESSED PATIENTS

These potential paths to recovery can lead to valuable strategies in working with severely depressed patients. However, as noted earlier, before the therapist can expect to be listened to, he must first help relieve the patient of his acute pain through the use of psychotropic medication or possibly electroconvulsive therapy. At the same time, the therapist should patiently attempt to establish contact with the patient by encouraging him to ventilate his feelings and by clearly demonstrating his own empathic response to them. The interest the therapist shows in the patient, and his willingness to understand his depression, in itself suggests to the patient that his illness is not hopeless. This interest is also supported by the therapist's concern to protect the patient from hurting or killing himself.

Later the therapist should urge the patient to try to reconstruct the sequence of events that preceded the onset of his depression so that he may better help him not only recover from his current illness but prevent or mitigate, as far as it is possible, future episodes. Aside from any biologic precipitants of the patient's illness, one frequently finds that a patient's depressive illness is precipitated by a specific constellation of circumstances to which he has fallen prey, and to which he has responded by becoming depressed. Such patients, for whom the precipitating conditions of their illness can be identified, can become forearmed and may be able to avoid situations which are psychologically toxic for them. Before psychotherapy, many of these patients live beyond their psychological means, repeatedly plunging into situations that almost certainly result in depression.

Imogene D., a 50-year-old divorced saleswoman, had been slipping deeper and deeper into a profound depression during a six- or seven-week period before her supervisor managed to convince her to see a psychiatrist. Although she had scarcely been able to do her work, she had managed at least to stay on the job on most days. When first seen, she was in severe distress and complained of "a great weight" on her chest. She had no appetite and had been sleeping poorly. She had no active suicidal thoughts but yearned to "go to sleep forever."

The doctor urged her to enter the hospital, but she refused. Fortunately, he was able to arrange for a young colleague of Mrs. D. to stay with her for a while, and she was given a week's supply of an antidepressant medication. She agreed not to harm herself while she was seeing the doctor and was told to call him at any hour at his office or at home if she felt the least urge to do so.

Initially, she refused to discuss her feelings and, when urged to do so, replied, "It doesn't do any good." "It does help, somehow, to talk about what you're thinking and feeling," the therapist replied. Over the next several weeks, the therapist encouraged Mrs. D. to explore with him the events that might have precipitated her depression. Piecemeal, she related that three months before her illness her only child, a daughter, had dropped out of college and gone off to live with a young man. She accused herself of having been the cause of this because she had been too lax with her daughter.

In a later session, Mrs. D. reported that some months prior to her daughter's departure she herself had had a brief love affair with a man 15 years younger than she, who had soon dropped her. She was intensely embarrassed in relating this to the therapist and looked obviously ashamed and guilty. "You look as if you expect me to hit you," he said. "I deserve everything that's coming to me," she replied. "How much more punishment do you think you must take?" "I don't know, but I feel that I'll never feel good about myself again." The therapist responded, "That would be a pity; you've already suffered a good deal. Would you give so much punishment to someone else?"

Over the next several months, Mrs. D.'s depression subsided very slowly. As she communicated more easily and felt less afraid of being judged, she raked up all manner of "wickedness" in her past. In fact, life had been very harsh to her: a broken family when she was very young; foster homes; a bad marriage; abandonment by her alcoholic husband; her own recent disastrous love affair; and finally her profound guilt and disappointment over her daughter's departure. The therapist thought he was beginning to understand some of the dynamics of Mrs. D.'s depression and made "interpretations" that related her past experiences to her present vulnerability to depression, but she merely looked baffled.

While the therapist grew concerned about the correctness of his interpretations, Mrs. D. was slowly but surely developing an intense positive transference to him, manifested by new, attractive clothes, a different hairstyle, and heavy perfume. The therapist finally became aware of what was happening and interpreted her behavior by saying, "You seem to be dressing up for me. I wonder if you want me to take the place of Bill [her young lover]?" Mrs. D. was furious and humiliated; she accused the therapist of having "a dirty mind" and trying to "twist" her thoughts. She became hysterical and could not be calmed. In desperation, the therapist recommended hospitalization, which she accepted. After six weeks in the hospital where she received medication and supportive and milieu therapy, Mrs. D. was discharged and she returned to work.

POSITIVE AND NEGATIVE APPROACHES

This clinical vignette illustrates, to some extent, what should and should not have been done. On the positive side, the therapist dealt with the patient's pain, he worked to protect her from self-destructive wishes, he acted as an auxiliary conscience—or superego—by showing her how much she had already suffered; he took her seriously and encouraged her to air her feelings; he struggled against her feelings of hopelessness. Throughout, he was a helping, caring person who systematically attempted to correct her distortions of the world around her as well as those she had about herself.

Some of this work, elaborated by Beck and others as cognitive psychotherapy, is an aspect of all forms of psychoanalytically oriented psychotherapy. What is at issue is the patient's misperceptions, misunderstandings, and distortions of inner and outer reality; it is a problem of ego function and relates not only to adequate or inadequate reality testing, but to the quality and nature of the feelings attached to the patient's experience of reality. Whether the therapist is dealing with a defense such as reaction formation, or a gross failure to appreciate reality, such as delusions or hallucinations, his work is to help the patient understand *what* he is doing, and then *how* it is adversely affecting his life; the *why* is often not dealt with in supportive psychotherapy.

Beyond the positive effect the therapist had on Mrs. D.'s depression were some negative consequences because he had not fully appreciated the fact that she apparently was not able to tolerate exploratory psychotherapy. Even when she was able to report important dynamic matters, she defended against making connections between them and could not accept the therapist's interpretations of them. Moreover, it seemed that the therapist's empathy failed him when he made his "transference" interpretation; although it *may* have been mistaken, it was *surely* ill-timed and unacceptable to the patient, who experienced it as judgmental and humiliating. Her relatively fragile ego broke down under what she experienced as an unbearable, hostile attack.

Depressed patients, because of their intense suffering, may lead a therapist to be overprotective and to "baby" a patient who needs encouragement to "get moving" in work and other activities. Other therapists react to their own urgent feelings of wanting to relieve pain and reassure by becoming harsh and peremptory. The patient's tenacious depressive posture may make the therapist feel guilty about his inability to make the patient well, or angry with him for not "cooperating." It is almost impossible for the therapist to hide these feelings from the patient, who sooner or later develops an uncanny sense of what the therapist is feeling. Needless to say, the therapist's own self-understanding is the key to preventing or rectifying potentially harmful countertransference reactions, whether working with depressed or any other patients.

THE SCHIZOPHRENIC PATIENT

A much more difficult problem of noncommunication can be seen with certain schizophrenic patients or those suffering from an acute non-specific psychosis. Their silence may result from a number of causes ranging from conscious negativism to catatonia. Any form of verbal interaction here is obviously unlikely and the therapist must rely almost entirely on what he sees: the patient's dress, hygiene, facial expressions, posture, body movements, gestures, and specific acts such as echopraxia (when the patient repeats the movements of someone else). In such circumstances, the mere presence for frequent short periods of time—five or ten minutes—of the therapist who greets the patient by name, repeats his own name, and perhaps does nothing more than sit with the patient is beneficial in that it tends to affirm their separateness.

On admission to the hospital, an otherwise unresponsive psychotic, middle-aged woman looked like a trapped animal. The therapist was unable to get her to describe her feelings or to say one word about anything until he said, "You look like you're about to jump out of your skin." The patient nodded affirmatively. "I want to help you. Is there something I can do?", he went on. "Water," the patient replied. That was the first word she had uttered in days, and it was all she was to say for some time, but a thin thread of contact had been established. The therapist who makes comments based on the patient's appearance, etc., must be careful not to seem magical or clairvoyant; his comments should be about the most obvious aspect of the patient.

THE PHOBIC PATIENT

The most effective barrier to communication between the therapist and the patient is, of course, the unwillingness or inability of the patient to come for treatment because of a crippling phobia. Many therapists become intensely concerned and frustrated when a patient whom they or someone else has advised to come for therapy refuses to do so. They are tempted, and occasionally succumb, to carry out one or another heroic measure, a step which may actually be "successful." These measures range from a useful visit to the patient's home to an inappropriate hospital commitment.

THE ROLE OF INSIGHT

Phobic patients are seen in all forms of therapy, but even in insight-oriented psychotherapy or in psychoanalysis—as Freud pointed out—the patient must ultimately confront the feared situation despite having grasped the psychological roots of his phobia. The anxiety is so great that insight by itself frequently seems insufficient; the patient is apparently unable to integrate that understanding into his psychological makeup so that his behavior will be adequately affected and altered. Until the patient can actually confront and experience the feared situation, the attendant anxiety will not begin to subside. To ignore the patient's current behavior and to focus uniquely on insight is to caricature insight-oriented psychotherapy and psychoanalysis as therapies which do not care about the patient's life just as long as he "understands" the dynamics of his behavior.

While it is true that insight is the cornerstone of these therapies, it has little value in itself, but becomes a potent force when it is integrated into the patient's psyche. Moreover, the understanding that effects change is not simply an intellectual grasp of a situation but an emotionally charged, cognitive experience that takes place when the patient relives his core neurotic conflicts and gives free play to his maladaptive character traits in the crucible of his transference relationship with the therapist.

BEHAVIOR MODIFICATION

Since this deeper form of understanding is generally not a goal of supportive psychotherapy, the therapist who deals with a phobic patient in that modality has definite limitations placed on his work. When he has fully dealt with the patient's cognitive misperceptions of the fear-inducing situation, he will usually find that a formal or informal behavior modification technique may be of great value. Many such techniques have been elaborated, attesting to the difficulties related to the cure of phobias. The therapist who sees phobic patients in supportive psychotherapy can either learn to utilize these techniques himself or may refer the patient to a therapist who is skilled in them. For those who wish to pursue these techniques further, a number of appropriate readings will be found in the list of references.

Agoraphobia, the fear of going outside one's house, represents the most challenging problem since this symptom keeps the patient from even going to the therapist. Fortunately, such a patient is usually able to leave his home if accompanied by a family member or a very close friend. This well-known observation becomes the key to the subsequent treatment.

Mr. Harry S. had been homebound for almost 15 years. His fear of leaving his parents' house seemed to have been precipitated by an attack of homosexual panic which occurred in his mid-twenties. At that time, he was hospitalized in a state hospital for about a year, discharged, and readmitted a few months later. The second hospitalization lasted about 20 months. During both hospitalizations, he was diagnosed as "chronic undifferentiated schizophrenia." A review of the hospital records, however, revealed no data that clearly supported such a diagnosis, regardless of the set of diagnostic criteria used.

When a community mental health center opened in his town, Mr. S.'s father inquired if his son, now almost 40 years old, could be seen as a patient. When he was told to send his son to the clinic for an evaluation, he said that Harry would never leave the house. Nevertheless, the next day the father accompanied his bewildered son to the clinic. The younger Mr. S. turned out to be a bright but extremely withdrawn man who was, however, closely in touch with reality and quite shrewd in many of his observations. At that time, the diagnosis of "inadequate personality" was made, and the goal of treatment agreed upon between Harry S. and his therapist was to enable him to leave his house in order that he might ultimately go to work. The need for some gainful occupation was becoming a critical issue because both his parents were in their seventies, of very modest means, and in deteriorating health.

For several months, the elder Mr. S. brought his son to the clinic every week, waited for the hour of therapy to be over, and then accompanied him home. When a reasonable degree of rapport had developed between the patient and the therapist, they began to work out a schedule to limit the amount of time the father spent accompanying his son to and from the clinic. At first the father began to let the patient walk the last two blocks to their house by himself, with the father walking a short distance behind him. Gradually this was increased until the patient was walking from the clinic to his home, with his father at a still greater distance from him; then the patient walked the last block by himself. At the end of a year, Mr. S. was able to go alone to and from the center.

When his therapist left the clinic and he was assigned to a new therapist, he suffered a recurrence of his agoraphobia. At this time, the new therapist, using the same technique as had been used before, was able to accelerate the process, and Mr. S. was soon able to navigate the course by himself. This patient later was able to attend a trade school where he learned a semiskilled occupation. Vocational rehabilitation services obtained work for him in a sheltered workshop which was located several miles from his home; he was able to go there daily, using public transportation.

AVOIDANCE OF STEREOTYPED EXPRESSIONS

It is not unusual to discover that a phobic patient has previously been to several other therapists and has "heard all that before." The therapist should be careful not to use stereotyped expressions or formulations which may lead to instant skepticism. In fact, therapists should generally avoid hackneyed expressions, even if they are "correct" and appropriate. So many psychiatric and psychoanalytic terms have entered into common, and frequently incorrect, usage that patients have an immediate sense that they are being pigeonholed into a diagnostic or dynamic category. I discussed this issue in Chapter IV, but it is especially relevant in relation to patients with phobias because very often they actually *have* heard it all before.

AVOIDANCE OF ANXIETY-PRODUCING SITUATIONS

It is useful with phobic patients, as it is to a greater or lesser extent with all patients, to help them to understand what kinds of situations or relationships are apt to provoke episodes of anxiety. This is really a "pedagogic" function of the therapist—another aspect of "ego building"—and can be of considerable help to the patient who often finds himself "over his head." In a similar way, the counterphobic patient who "rushes in where wise men fear to tread" can be shown what he is doing and how he repeatedly gets burned in the process. As I have pointed out, patients can sometimes become exceptionally sensitive to what are, for them at least, "toxic" situations which they can then avoid.

A good adaptation to the world includes an awareness of the kinds of situations and relationships which are harmful to an individual. Most people, from the fund of their experience, intuitively develop a sense of what is good or bad for them. They may have some mild conflict about certain situations, but for the most part they act in ways that over time are the most gratifying and the least painful. Obviously, this refers to situations over which they exercise some reasonable control. However, many patients seem to lack the ability to avoid those situations which are harmful to them and which may provoke a relapse of their illness. This tends to occur frequently with patients in supportive psychotherapy because of their difficulties in control of impulses, erratic judgment, problems with reality testing, and social inexperience. It is, therefore, of considerable value to these patients to help them learn which situations to avoid.

WARNING SYMPTOMS

Moreover, these patients should be helped to become aware of the earliest signs of the onset of illness, even though these warning signs are subtle and the onset insidious. Such signals differ from one individual to another, and each patient ought to become attuned to his own. These commonly include: sleep difficulties—especially when these are progressive, and comprise excessive sleeping as well as problems with insomnia; frequent, intense, and progressively longer lasting episodes of anxiety; restlessness; changes in eating habits; difficulty in concentration; changes in sexual habits and sexual drive; progressive irrascibility, argumentativeness, temper tantrums, and physical violence; changes in work habits; social withdrawal, isolation; and "letting oneself go" in general appearance and dress.

Patients who become sensitive to those situations that are harmful to them, as well as to the changes within themselves which are harbingers of regression, can often take appropriate measures to forestall a relapse. At the very least they know when to return to their therapist for help.

THE MASOCHISTIC PATIENT

It is difficult to help an individual who enjoys his suffering—usually described as masochistic. Since his psychological makeup utilizes pain to achieve pleasure, it is obvious that attempts to help this patient are often frustrated. The therapist who wants to be a helper to this patient soon discovers that the patient does not really want to be helped, at least not in the manner which the therapist has in mind. What is worse, he may reject the therapist's assumption of the role of helper and accuse him of being an enemy. The therapist thus finds himself regarded as sadistic, humiliating and insulting, unsympathetic, interested only in his work, money, leisure activities and not at all in the patient. These accusations tend to have a painful effect on most therapists since they would like to be the opposite of the way the patient experiences them.

Although masochism has many determinants, a common manifestation is an apparent defense of the weak, the oppressed, the isolated—who otherwise feel unable to deal with whomever they identify as their oppressor. If the weak individual (or group) senses that there are shared values—kindness, empathy, support, etc.—between his oppressor and himself, he will tax his "enemy" with his failure to be true to those values, regardless of whether the enemy is so or not. In treating his therapist as if he were a heartless scoundrel, the masochistic patient is actually using his weakness as a Trojan horse to carry out an attack on the therapist. In effect, he uses his masochistic position sadistically.

Miss Margaret C., a 35-year-old single nurse had been seeing a therapist for several months. She had originally presented herself for treatment on the advice of her supervisor who felt that Miss C. had not "fitted into" the ward staff with whom she worked. For the most part, the patient continued to protest that she was being treated badly by her colleagues who, she felt, regarded her as a snobbish outsider.

Much of the treatment at first had centered on the therapist's attempt to have Miss C. gain some emotional distance from her relationships with other people, and to see what responsibility she might have for her daily abrasive encounters with them. One day, the therapist was feeling particularly provoked by Miss C.; every time he tried to explore an area of difficulty which she had reported, she rebuffed and contradicted him. His anger was beginning to show. "You're so predictable," she exclaimed. "*You're* always right, and *I'm* always wrong. Why don't you admit it? It's clear, you hate my guts. The best thing I can do is go home and turn on the gas—then you won't have me on your hands anymore."

She started gathering up her things to leave. The therapist was furious because he realized not only that at that moment he *was* very angry with Miss C. but also that she had seen his anger; he was both frightened by her suicidal threat and ashamed of his hostile feelings. Unable to respond thoughtfully, he sputtered and finally shouted, "Close the door and come back here!" Miss C. was alarmed at his visible rage, but did resume her seat. "It looks like even you, too, lose your cool," she finally said. "Yes," the therapist replied. "You've consistently regarded me as your enemy: you tell me over and over again that I have no feelings, that I hate you, and wish you were dead. I'm sorry I yelled at you, but despite what you might think, I too have feelings. Whether you are aware of it or not, I think you have tried to hurt me. When you behave like this with other people, they aren't interested in understanding why you act that way; they either retaliate or walk away from you. Here at least we can work on this and try to understand why you have to behave in ways that make people angry with you."

Later Miss C. admitted that, having "drawn blood," she was afraid that the therapist would probably refuse to continue to see her. She had been surprised and gratified that he had not rejected her. In some ways, it may have been useful for this patient to see that someone whom she respected was able to get angry, calm down, and continue to work with her without resentment. For his part, that evening the therapist did some self-analytic "homework" to better understand his loss of control. It would have been facile for him to ascribe it to a simple reaction to the patient's provocations. Rather, as he thought more about it, and about a dream he had the night before the therapy hour just described, he was able to understand that his countertransference had had more than one determinant to it.

STRUCTURAL AND OBJECT RELATIONS

To bring about significant structural changes is difficult in all forms of psychotherapy, but it is more so in supportive work because the patient's difficulties are largely in the area of structural *deficits* rather than problems in the *function* of these structures. Because of the patient's relative immaturity, countertransference reactions may be very intense; the therapist wants to feel empathic towards the patient but he is rejected; he wants to understand him, but finds him an enigma; he wants to "cure" the patient but, to his chagrin, he discovers that he can consider it a therapeutic triumph merely to have prevented the patient's further regression. The therapist's own unresolved yearnings to "heal all, know all and love all" come headlong into conflict with the patient's desires and needs. Perhaps nothing stands in his way more than the patient's inability to form an "object relationship" with him, that is, to develop a positive emotional investment in his therapist.

Psychotherapists debate whether the growth of object relatedness in a patient in whom it is deficient can occur. I believe that there are some patients in whom such a development can and does take place in the course of extended psychotherapy. Certainly, the possibilities for the growth of object relations are stronger if the patient has already demonstrated in his past some potential in this area, even if it has been only an attachment to a pet.

What the therapist can best do to foster the development of object relations is to present himself as a model with whom the patient can identify. If the therapist is generally empathic, supportive of the patient's self-esteem, flexible, dedicated to his work (punctual, consistent, etc.), not retaliatory or punitive, and not judgmental, he will surely be markedly different from almost everyone else in the patient's life. He is apt to be liked, admired, and respected by the patient who then may begin, even if in a modest way, to model the therapist.

Such a process may represent a deep identification or may be only a superficial imitation. Indeed, the first indication that a genuine identification might have begun is often seen in the form of imitation: wearing a similar article of clothing, repeating certain gestures or phrases, etc. But even if the imitation remains at that level, that is, not integrated firmly into the patient's personality, it can be useful.

The therapist can do no more than strive toward this end; he should be deeply gratified if even slight changes occur; and he should not be disappointed if his efforts are mostly unsuccessful because, in trying to influence an individual's object relatedness, the therapist is grappling with a human phenomenon whose roots go back to the earliest months of a patient's life.

In this, and the previous three chapters, I have described some common problems encountered in supportive psychotherapy and have given some suggestions for dealing with them therapeutically. These problems and the technical suggestions for dealing with them are meant to be representative of the kinds of situations the psychotherapist encounters in doing supportive psychotherapy, although many of the situations are dealt with in all forms of therapy.

In supportive treatment, adaptive change is sought while maintaining the deeply repressed sources of the symptoms, in contrast to insight-oriented treatment where efforts are directed to uncovering those hidden roots. As long as the therapist has grasped the essential differences and goals of these two modalities of treatment, he will be able to deal effectively with new problems as they arise. His greatest assets will always be his dynamic understanding, flexibility, and empathy; when these are allied with experience, the therapist can find supportive psychotherapy richly rewarding.

14

The Place of the Dream
in Supportive Psychotherapy

Since the publication of Freud's *Interpretation of Dreams* in 1900, the dream has been inextricably linked to psychotherapy. Although dream interpretation originally arose in psychoanalytic practice as a means of learning more about a patient's unconscious processes, to some degree it is now part of all dynamic psychotherapies. However, of the large body of literature dealing with the use of the dream, there is remarkably little concerned with the dream in psychotherapy generally—compared to psychoanalysis—and still less in supportive psychotherapy specifically.

This lack is but one more indication of the general neglect of supportive psychotherapy—a situation that has evolved into a failure to base the practice of this form of treatment on carefully formulated principles and a failure to derive appropriate techniques from them. The lack of a systematic approach to supportive psychotherapy has thus led to confusion, often resulting in an imitation in supportive treatment of techniques intended to be used in psychoanalysis or in insight-oriented psychotherapy.

Precisely because the dream is the royal road to the unconscious, as Freud called it, there are very good reasons why a therapist might not choose to follow that road, as far as possible, in supportive psychotherapy, in direct contrast to what might be pursued in insight-oriented psychotherapy. In the latter form of treatment, the patient is considered able to tolerate some degree of regression for the purposes of the therapeutic process; the frequency of meetings allows time for a detailed study of a patient's dreams and of other material, especially that which relates to the fostered transference. There is an understanding by the therapist or analyst and by the patient, that a fairly lengthy period of time will be devoted to the therapeutic process.

These conditions do not prevail in supportive psychotherapy, in which regression is to be avoided, and the frequency and often the duration of meetings between therapist and patient are carefully limited. Furthermore, the goal in supportive psychotherapy is not to make conscious (to uncover) as much as possible of what has been unconscious. In patients with severe psychological deficits and deficiencies, and in most psychotic patients, it is unwise to break down those already enfeebled defensive operations which serve to keep painful or abhorrent material out of awareness and protect the patient from a total psychological breakdown. In fact, as has been shown, when these defense functions are fragile, specific efforts must be made in supportive psychotherapy to shore them up.

At the outset of supportive treatment, I do not think it is generally advisable to request that the patient report his dreams. Explorations of the dreams may facilitate the emergence of unconscious material that should best remain out of awareness. However, if the patient spontaneously reports a dream, it should be acknowledged as a valid and valued contribution. The patient can then simply be asked if he has had any thoughts about the dream, and the matter can remain there. There is truth in the cliché that the dream has been offered to the therapist as a gift and to ignore it might, with justification, be considered as unappreciative or rude.

Insofar as the therapist is able to reach some understanding of the dreams of patients in supportive psychotherapy, he does so by using the same processes as would be applicable in understanding the dreams of patients in any other form of treatment: that is, the therapist listens both to what the patient says directly about the dream and to anything else in the hour which can be regarded as an association to the dream, and he attempts to insert the dream into the patient's psychological life at that particular time. This is a silent process.

The central consideration concerns what is told to the patient. In supportive psychotherapy, in general, the therapist's comments about the dream should relate it to the "surface" of the patient's mental life at that point, both in or out of the therapy hour. No attempts to interpret the dream in regard to unconscious processes are made. What should guide the therapist in determining what he should communicate to the patient is a consideration of what will serve the specific therapeutic goals. Typically, in supportive psychotherapy, the therapist will seek to strengthen more adaptive and less pathological ego defenses; he will support better reality testing, control of impulses, enhancement of object relations, and tolerance of anxiety and depressive feelings.

For example, a "borderline" patient, whose prominent tendency to use projection was creating serious difficulties for him at work, had the following dream: "I was being chased by my boss who was carrying a big knife; I was really scared. Just when I thought he would catch up with me, I woke up." The patient immediately associated this to a current fantasy that his employer disliked him and was "out to get him." By reminding the patient that the dream was his own "production," the therapist was able to relate the patient's need to see his employer as menacing in order not to feel his own hostility toward his employer. At the same time this offered the therapist the opportunity to look at the patient's fears of him and to strengthen their relationship.

The therapist also attempts to foster the therapeutic relationship by avoiding deep interpretations of unconscious material which deal, for example, with transference and by limiting himself to "upward" interpretations relating to the patient's conscious and preconscious attitudes toward the therapist as a real person. This approach helps the patient to accept the therapist as a helper. Dreams with an erotic content about the therapist, for example, can be "interpreted" in this way by explaining the erotic content as representing feelings of friendliness and gratitude. This not only strengthens the therapeutic relationship, but also helps keep out of awareness thoughts that might prove to be overwhelming to the patient. It can also strengthen the patient's defenses of repression, intellectualization and rationalization—all of which are more adaptive than projection or denial.

In some patients with severe ego deficits, weak functions such as reality testing can be supported by appropriate "interpretations." A "borderline" college student with strong unconscious homosexual tendencies frequently complained that various men were trying to seduce him. He reported the following dream: "I was walking across the campus when I saw a huge bird sitting on some steps. The bird had a long, menacing beak. I was thinking of running but I was afraid the bird would fly after me. I decided to play it cool and not appear frightened. When I got closer, I saw that the bird was only a stone statue." This dream became a useful vehicle to deal with the patient's faulty perception of the "seducing men" he saw around him by showing him that things are not always what we first believe them to be. The dream also lent itself to dealing with the patient's poor impulse control by using it as an object lesson demonstrating the value of delaying action.

The dream can be used to modulate the influence of an archaic superego—that is, the harsh conscience of a child. To a schizophrenic patient who dreamed that he was beating his neighbor's dog, the therapist commented, "It seems natural that you might think of beating the dog because you were angry with your neighbor, but you wouldn't actually act to do him any harm."

By putting the dream into the context of the patient's psychological life, the therapist suspected that the dream might relate to oedipal displacement, transference issues, homosexual wishes, and masturbatory guilt. However, he specifically avoided these matters, and his comment offered the patient a rationalization of his hostility which may have helped repress conflicts with which the patient was having difficulty dealing. He also suggested that hostile *thoughts* are permissible, in contrast to violent *acts*; he may have helped diminish anxiety and guilt; and he clearly strengthened the patient-therapist relationship by demonstrating to the patient that he was listening and trying to understand him.

Other than asking these patients for general thoughts relating to their dreams, it is not advisable to ask for or encourage free association because it may foster further regression, primary process thinking, and even uncontrolled behavior. Needless to say, the therapist may be inclined to shift his posture towards a deeper understanding of the dream, as of any other material produced by the patient, if there is evidence that the patient can tolerate slightly deeper interpretations and is perhaps moving in the direction of beginning to do some insight-oriented work.

The dream may also function in supportive psychotherapy, as in other forms of therapy, as the chorus in a Greek drama—that is, it can be understood as a commentary on the therapeutic situation, reflecting both conscious and unconscious reactions to therapy and the therapist. This can be of great help to the therapist who might become aware that the patient is experiencing him as coercive, manipulative, judgmental, demeaning, callous, inquisitorial, or seductive.

Although it would appear that the therapist might be placing an undue reliance on the manifest content of the dream, he is actually using the entire therapeutic situation as an association to the dream. If the therapist believes the dream is a commentary on his behavior, he should begin to review his interaction with the patient during the hours preceeding the dream in order to determine to what extent the patient's feelings correspond to actual events or to distortions.

For example, a patient dreamed that a doctor was giving him a series of enemas. The therapist reviewed several previous hours and became aware that he had been making unrealistic demands of this very fragile patient. If the patient's perceptions seem to be essentially correct, such knowledge can lead not only to healthy changes in the therapist's work, but even to his open acknowledgment, under certain circumstances, of the correctness of the patient's thoughts. This in turn can lead to a firmer rapport between them and to the development of a deeper trust.

The therapist should be particularly alerted to dreams in which the patient sees himself as being pushed, pulled, tugged, intruded upon in any manner, suffering, or sexually attacked. The graphic representations of these feelings in dreams may take many forms, and the therapist himself will have to associate to them since he should not plan on having the patient do so. This can serve as an excellent corrective of one's therapeutic posture.

Thus, although dream interpretation plays a very small role in supportive psychotherapy and might even be nonexistent, it is possible for it to be useful in the fundamental sense of supporting weak ego functions, diminishing the most pathological behavior and psychological processes, and enhancing more adaptive modes of acting and experiencing. Furthermore, studying these dreams can enhance the therapist's professional growth.

15

Changing from Supportive
to Insight-Oriented Psychotherapy

During the course of supportive psychotherapy, evidence may accumulate which makes the therapist aware of particular changes in his patient, as well as in the therapeutic process itself, that suggest that a shift to an explorative, insight-oriented form of treatment is possible. Is such a change desirable, if it is in fact feasible? The answer is clearly in the affirmative.

If supportive treatment is fundamentally a substitutive and at times ego strengthening process, then it follows that if a patient is able to do explorative, "uncovering" work, he has probably made some important steps in overcoming the ego deficits or weaknesses that brought him into treatment in the first place. It means that his ego functions may have become sufficiently developed to permit some insight work to take place. Theoretically and practically, the therapist can now expect that, at least to some extent, resistances can be modified, a transference allowed to develop, unconscious material can be interpreted, etc. In human terms, this suggests that the patient may now be able to more fully enrich his life in a variety of areas: work, love, relationships, sublimations, and inner emotional harmony.

REASONS FOR FAULTY EVALUATION

Before the therapist decides that changes have occurred which indicate the possibility of a transition to insight-oriented psychotherapy, he should ask himself whether the original decision to begin supportive psychotherapy may have been incorrect because of a faulty evaluation; that is, did the patient actually have greater ego strength than was at first evident? Outside of a therapist's inexperience or inability to do a careful evaluation, there are a number of situations which can lead even an able clinician astray. The most frequent possibility is that the patient appears more disturbed than he really is because he is reacting to a recent stressful occurrence; and his current mental status is due to a temporary regression and does not represent a lifelong deficiency in psychological development.

Adolescents may seem far more disturbed than they really are because of emotional volatility and frequent and sometimes significant fluctuations in ego functioning. Drug and alcohol abusers and individuals who have recently suffered from important organic illness may also appear to be deeply debilitated psychologically. Those who have undergone a major loss—of someone dear to them, of their job, social status or reputation—may appear to have long-standing emotional and developmental problems. Similarly, profound humiliation or an intense guilt reaction following some actual behavior by the patient may distort the clinical picture. In general, such distortions can be seen after any sort of trauma—real, symbolic, or fantasied.

All of these conditions can lead the evaluating therapist to conclude that the patient is not an appropriate candidate for insight-oriented psychotherapy. Later on, when the impact of the trauma or loss has subsided, the patient's strength may become more evident to the therapist, and a change in the mode of psychotherapeutic work becomes possible.

Some patients, in their desire to receive treatment, have the idea that they will be accepted for treatment only if they look very sick. Hysterical patients, who can be especially dramatic, may also appear to the interviewer as much more disturbed than they really are. Patients who have been brought against their will to the therapist may seem to be totally unmotivated for any form of psychotherapy, but this resistance may represent hostility more to the family member who brought them than to the treatment process itself. In an effort to gratify certain masochistic impulses, through early resistance to treatment or out of feelings of unworthiness, some individuals may initially seem unable to tolerate explorative psychotherapy.

REASONS FOR CHANGE

What causes a patient to change who initially presented with genuine developmental deficits? I can only offer some presumptive reasons, not in order of importance, but largely based on our knowledge of human development in general. Perhaps the most important factor consists of the identifications the patient may develop with his therapist during a relatively prolonged contact between them. The precondition for such identifications lies in the positive feelings the patient has experienced towards his therapist. Such pervasively positive feelings grow out of a therapeutic atmosphere in which the patient feels respected, valued, taken seriously, responded to empathically, and not judged. It is likely that such an environment, even though it is never ideal, is in marked contrast to what the patient experienced as a child and even in adult life.

From such an essentially benevolent matrix, the patient may consciously and unconsciously identify with a number of psychological traits in the therapist. These traits, though general and relatively few in number, can lead to gratifying changes in the patient, even if they develop only to a modest extent. The most common characteristic consists of the therapist's devotion to his work and therefore to the patient, and his manifest desire and ability to maintain a consistent approach to the patient, almost regardless of how the patient treats him. Repeatedly, this shows the patient that a human being can commit himself to another person and need not reject him because of some error in that person's ways. This tends to help the patient to modulate his need to "split" people into saints and sinners.

The therapist is also firm in his commitment to observable, everyday reality. Although he entertains and appreciates fantasy and illusion, he consistently distinguishes them from what can be perceived. He admits to obvious mistakes on his part—forgetting an appointment, for example—and shows the patient that he is fallible, that he makes no pretense at being perfect, and can tolerate being "only" a human being. He struggles repeatedly with the patient to have him *think* about behavioral acts before he commits them; he demonstrates how it is in the patient's interest to delay impulses until he has thought them through; by his own thoughtful, considered behavior, he also gives the patient a model of self-control with which to identify. By his flexibility in all his dealings with the patient, the therapist demonstrates the mal-adaptiveness of the patient's rigid and stereotyped reactions to people and events. Finally, his empathic attitude helps the patient feel that he is understood and respected; this in turn may permit him to begin to respond similarly to the people around him.

Beyond the identifications that may occur, the therapist engages in ongoing clarifications of the patient's maladaptive behavior. For example, he shows the patient his typical self-destructive patterns and their unfortunate consequences. He encourages the patient to seek adult gratifications, ideally in socially and personally acceptable ways. He shows the patient how such behavior enhances his self-esteem and satisfies and modulates his sexual and aggressive impulses. By his flexibility in all his dealings with the patient, the therapist supports, guides, and tries to develop the patient's autonomy. The patient begins to see that if he becomes more autonomous it does not mean that he will lose the support of his therapist. He discovers that acts and decisions, formerly feared, are much less frightening in actual experience than in fantasy. At the same time, he sees that he can, for example, share his positive, perhaps even loving, feelings towards the therapist without being disgustedly pushed away or taken in, engulfed, and reduced to nothingness.

CHANGES IN REALITY TESTING

The following changes include some of the positive developments that suggest that a shift to an insight-oriented form of treatment may be indicated. Perhaps the most important is the patient's progressively more objective assessment of unpleasant reality; he distorts the external and inner worlds less and tends more to believe "his own eyes." Stressful situations provoke less regression and those episodes that do occur are less frequent, shorter, and not as profound as previously.

DECREASED DENIAL, PROJECTION, SPLITTING

Closely related to improved reality testing is the decreased use of such defenses as denial, projection, and splitting. The patient in whom such changes occur usually begins by recognizing that although he has continued to utilize these defenses, he is able to recognize what he has done, at least after the fact. For example, he may see that he has ascribed his hostile thoughts to someone else, or he may become able to concede that someone who was curt with him has also shown him kindness.

Reciprocally, the therapist may see that the patient is better able to tolerate his own shortcomings and can maintain a more positive image of himself; and when he has done something he doesn't like, he is less despairing and self-punitive. Of course, the best arena to work through the most maladaptive behavior is in the patient's relationship with the therapist who patiently, repeatedly (over years, if need be), and empathically corrects the patient's distortions of him. Again, such corrections are best obtained in practice not by contradicting the patient's views, but by the therapist's demonstrating their incorrectness by his own behavior.

In the more successful situation, these defenses gradually become increasingly alien to the patient. Although he at first continues to utilize them and is only able to identify them afterwards, he may learn to recognize them *while* he is denying, projecting, or splitting. The therapist will strive to enable the patient to catch himself on the verge of using these defenses and being able to avoid doing so altogether.

IMPROVEMENT IN OBJECT RELATIONSHIPS

Related to improved reality testing and to the decreased use of projection and splitting is an improvement in the patient's object relationships. The therapist may begin to hear that a relationship—new or preexisting—seems to be on a sounder footing: there are fewer fluctuations in the patient's feelings towards the other person and there are expressions of warmth, affection, tenderness, and concern for the other. In some patients there is less promiscuity or less frequent dropping of friends, fewer and milder fights, etc. In his relationship with the therapist, the patient seems less hostile and more tolerant of vacations or occasional changed appointments, suggesting that he has a firmer, more enduring mental representation of the therapist as a helping, benevolent individual, which survives even physical separation.

IMPROVED IMPULSE CONTROL

When patients with a previous history of destructive and self-destructive impulses begin to evolve, they may engage less frequently in such behavior and be better able to delay the urge to act on an aggressive or sexual impulse; they may find another, more acceptable path toward gratification. When the therapist, an external source of control, has set clear limits on the patient's behavior and is explicit as to what is and is not acceptable, he helps the patient to identify with such limit setting. One may hope that this delaying and limit setting may become, at least to some extent, part of the patient's character structure.

SUBLIMATION

Finally, the therapist should be attentive to information that suggests that the patient is developing new or extending previous areas of sublimation. Usually this is reflected in an improved work or school performance. This may take the form of feelings of pleasure related to the work, improved relations with peers and authority figures, or advancement and promotion. Additionally, the patient may report on hobbies, social activities, athletics or other leisure time activity.

RECOGNIZING IMPROVEMENT

One should realize that patients do not always tell their therapists about improvement in their behavior. Consciously or unconsciously, they may be concerned that the therapist will terminate therapy if he learns of such changes. In some instances, in his anger with the therapist, a patient may not want to give him the pleasure of learning of his improvement; however, sooner or later, information will usually emerge. When it does, I believe it is useful for the therapist to acknowledge whatever concrete steps the patient is taking to enrich his life. This does not require lengthy compliments, but some recognition and approval is therapeutic and human. For example, a very constricted or socially isolated patient may make a hesitant move into the outside world, a move that might be awkward or even inappropriate. In such situations, it is important for the therapist to recognize that what is useful and significant is simply that the patient has *done* something, and not to focus on the result of the attempt. To be critical of him at this point might deter the patient from going forward with a further exploration of his potential.

The changes described obviously vary in degree and may be only "more or less" present. As in the initial evaluation, the therapist should be careful not to take any single factor by itself as decisive, but to consider it as part of a general reassessment which explores the same issues that were covered in the first evaluation.

CHANGING FROM SUPPORTIVE THERAPY

When the therapist is reasonably convinced that sufficient changes have taken place, he should slowly attempt to establish a therapeutic environment that is somewhat in between the supportive and explorative forms. The patient may by permitted a little greater latitude in regression in the hour, for example, in terms of transference manifestations; but this should be regulated and allowed to develop more fully in a piecemeal, controlled manner.

The therapist himself should only gradually permit the patient to assume a larger role in the hour. It is awkward, jolting, and perplexing to the patient if the therapist abruptly changes his stance. He can, however, bridge the two modes of therapy by increasing his "facilitating," neutral remarks ("Tell me some more about that," "I see," "Uh huh," etc.) while he decreases his specifically supportive comments. If he "holds" the patient in this gray area, between supportive and insight-oriented treatment, he can with reasonable effectiveness guide the situation in such a way as to move forward in as deliberate a way as possible.

The patient need not be formally told that such a change in the mode of treatment is being made. However, if he should remark on the changes in the therapist's behavior, the therapist can acknowledge this perception and tell the patient that he seems to have developed a greater ability to look at himself, and in greater depth; as a result, the therapist thinks it would be useful for the patient to speak his mind—his thoughts and feelings—more freely; and together, patient and therapist will try to better understand these thoughts and feelings.

During this time, much like during the initial evaluation, the therapist may make one or two interpretations of modest "depth" to assess the patient's current psychological-mindedness. One pitfall that may occur consists of the patient's ability to seem insightful, even though such understanding may only reflect his ability to intellectualize. Such a possibility can at times lead to an inappropriate initial assignment of a patient to insight-oriented psychotherapy, as well as prompting the therapist to change to that mode after supportive work has gone on for some time.

SHIFTING FROM INSIGHT-ORIENTED PSYCHOTHERAPY

This last consideration leads me to deal briefly with the occasional necessity of shifting from insight-oriented to supportive psychotherapy. Such a change is usually the result of one or the other of two situations. The first is the relatively frequent but temporary need during insight-oriented therapy to support a patient who has been overwhelmed by some intercurrent, traumatic event, especially a powerful external stress such as the loss of a close relative, divorce, loss of a job, expulsion from school, or life-threatening physical illness. Occasionally, the stress may occur within therapy itself and be the result of an especially stressful interpretation or of a markedly painful insight. These situations may have long-lasting effects, but most of them are transitory and the patient can be carried through with only a minimum of support and a return to insight-oriented work can be effected before long.

The other situation is not fundamentally related to a particular stress although it may be provoked by one. It concerns the initial evaluation itself when a patient was erroneously assessed as an appropriate candidate for insight-oriented psychotherapy. These are the situations in which the evaluating therapist overlooked or, because of inexperience, was unable to identify significant ego deficits in the patient which would contraindicate explorative therapy, at least until significant progress towards ego building had taken place. If the therapist becomes concerned that he has erred by attributing greater ego strength to the patient than seems warranted, he should be reasonably sure that the patient does, in fact, have important ego deficiencies and is not simply showing the characteristic behavior due to a regression that is actually provoked by a powerful stress either in therapy or arising in the environment.

When the therapist is convinced that the initial assessment was faulty, he should plan on moving to a supportive, ego-substitutive mode of treatment. It is possible, regardless of one's assessment of the regression as transient or otherwise, that after some time the therapist may see that the patient has stabilized, that his intense anxiety and/or depression have diminished, and that once again he seems able to tolerate insight-oriented treatment. In such a situation, some exploration can carefully be resumed.

There is no reason why shifts cannot take place several times in the course of several years of psychotherapy. In fact, I believe they do occur, and probably far more frequently than many therapists either realize or acknowledge. Many therapists seem to respond appropriately but rather more intuitively than cognitively to these changing needs. For the beginning therapist, it is better that he not rely on intuition but that he proceed from an ongoing "monitoring" of the therapeutic process along the lines suggested. The critical instruments are the therapist's perception of the state of the patient's ego at any given time and his own flexibility in being able to move in whatever direction would be most beneficial to the patient.

For a variety of reasons, ranging from the personality of the therapist to factors in the patient, it may not always be expedient or comfortable for the therapist to shift the mode of treatment with a given patient. In such situations, he should give serious consideration to transferring the patient to another therapist. This too may not be a simple task, and so the therapist must balance the advantages against the disadvantages in treating the patient himself when he believes it useful to change to a different type of treatment.

16

Auxiliary Supportive Measures

Although I have focused on the psychotherapeutic aspect of supportive work, it is important to bear in mind that whether or not the patient is literally in therapy there are a number of additional means of helping him. Paradoxically, this reminder is perhaps more applicable to patients who are seen in frequent, regularly scheduled appointments because the therapist can easily develop the illusion that they spend a good deal of time with him, when in reality it represents a very small part of the patients' life. In contrast, one recognizes that the individual who does not see a therapist at all, or very infrequently, is *fully* dependent on "outside" sources for help.

Since the major effort in supportive psychotherapy is to provide what is lacking in ego functions or to enhance what is only insufficiently present, the therapist should avail himself of all the resources at his disposal which may provide support to all the patients he is treating and even to those who are not his patients but whose lives he can influence to some extent.

FAMILY AND FRIENDS

The commonest source of support is found in the patient's own family and close friends. Under special circumstances, the therapist may seek the cooperation of people who are further removed from the patient, such as neighbors, other residents in a nursing home, or fellow inmates in a prison. These individuals can serve in a wide variety of ways of which perhaps the most useful is to act as a reasonably objective barometer of the patient's well-being in general, and of his mental status in particular. Those who are closest to the patient are sometimes the best and not infrequently the only people able to perceive the beginning signs of regression.

Admittedly, it is well known that it may be just those who are closest to the patient who are the most apt to deny regressive developments in him and gloss over what might be significant evidence of deterioration. Another potential disadvantage of family support is that while the family members may be of service to the patient, they may also subtly undermine the patient's psychological stability by simply repeating the kind of behavior which earlier had had an injurious effect on the patient's psychological development and fostered his emotional difficulties. In these cases, it is helpful for the family to be counseled or seen along with the patient in some form of family therapy. The therapist should carefully observe the interaction between the individuals and the patient to determine whether the relationship is truly supportive.

The family can help the patient test reality, pointing out fallacies in his perceptions when these occur. The family may be able to set limits on destructive or other maladaptive behavior. They can learn how to reward the patient for activities which are adaptive and further the development of independence and maturity. When the patient begins to regress, they can encourage him to visit a mental health professional at what might be the onset of a potentially deep regression, in order to minimize its progression. If a mild regression is evident, the family may often be able to keep the patient at home and provide him with useful, supportive care. At their best, the family and intimate friends can shore up the patient's crumbling ego functions as well as provide the attention, care, and love which perhaps only someone closely connected to him can provide.

Obviously, for many reasons, they usually are unable to take care of the patient in the course of a serious illness. At such times, they may find themselves materially or emotionally unable to manage the patient; he may be so regressed that only skilled professionals can help him, or he may be violent, suicidal, or homicidal. In these situations, voluntary or involuntary hospitalization is mandatory. In all such instances, it is essential to explain to the patient why hospitalization must be carried out and to encourage the patient to express how he feels about it and ask any questions regarding the need to put him in the hospital. Since hospitalization combines both psychotherapeutic and auxiliary supportive measures, I shall briefly discuss it in this chapter.

WORKING WITH HOSPITALIZED PATIENTS

When supportive psychotherapy is carried out with hospitalized patients it is of relatively short duration—rarely more than two months, the duration of the stay in the hospital. Therapy may also have begun prior to admission and may well continue following discharge.

In the hospital, supportive treatment generally follows the same principles as outpatient treatment, the principal difference being that the patient's condition is usually more aggravated. He frequently may have been admitted because of a relatively severe and acute regression—that is, as the result of a crisis of some sort. He may have been hospitalized for the treatment of alcohol or drug addiction; he may be actively suicidal or homicidal; he may be suffering from severe manic-depressive illness, recurrent schizophrenia, a nonspecific psychosis, a psychosomatic illness, or an organic brain syndrome. On the other hand, many patients in the hospital do not have an acute illness, but have been hospitalized because their mental condition had gradually deteriorated to the point where they needed more intensive treatment and/or separation from their family for a period of time.

Patients who are involuntarily admitted to the hospital are usually unable to control their destructive impulses, whether these be directed to themselves or to others. The first task is for the staff to supply that control for the patient who may be suffering from an acute schizophrenic episode, a depression with the hostility directed toward himself, or mania. These patients should always be dealt with in as humane a way as any other patient: they should be told that they will receive care and that the staff will and must protect them from inflicting injury on themselves or others. Adequate psychotropic medication, seclusion, restraints if absolutely necessary—and these for only as long as warranted—should be introduced.

Most patients are grateful for such imposed limits, despite complaints to the contrary. It is usually painful for an individual to feel overwhelmed by his impulses—something like being at the wheel of a car that is skidding across an ice-covered road. The sooner the therapist can enter into a relationship with the patient, the sooner he can become a point of attachment for the patient. Often, with several staff members who rotate through two or three shifts, the therapist becomes the only fixed point on the patient's confusing horizon. During this early acute phase, the therapist should be thoroughly "real" for the patient in every way possible in order to strengthen the patient's debilitated reality testing.

In many ways supportive psychotherapy with the hospitalized patient can be more effective than with the outpatient because the patient's entire day can be more or less structured. It is the absence of effective structure in the lives of many chronic mental patients, among other factors, that makes working with them particularly difficult. The therapist may spend an hour or so each month with the outpatient who, in the rest of his time can be idle, withdraw from the people around him, engage in impulsive behavior, or be destructive. In contrast, while the residential treatment situation is not ideal, it may optimally provide some structure, set limits, and foster attempts to mobilize the patient to engage in sublimatory activities of which there is usually no lack: occupational and recreational therapies, group activities of various sorts, etc.

There is a tendency for the conscientious therapist to spend what may be excessive amounts of time with hospitalized patients—excessive because frequent and relatively lengthy visits tend to promote unwanted transference reactions and may lead to a highly dependent relationship. It is generally useful for the therapist to schedule therapy interviews with these patients only somewhat more often than he would if he were seeing the patient outside the hospital. To counteract the relative increase in frequency of meetings, their duration can be shortened. Two or three therapy sessions a week, lasting 15 to 20 minutes, seem optimal. On the other days, the therapist can spend five minutes or less with the patient to maintain contact. In general, these visits can be utilized to acquaint the therapist with the patient's current mental status, modifications in his daily activities and his feelings about them. Visits also provide the patient with the opportunity to talk about his relationship with other staff members, etc.

The hospital setting provides the therapist with a full range of auxiliary ego-supporting individuals such as social workers, nurses, occupational and recreational therapists, and house-staff officers. The team approach has proven to be of great value for most hospitalized patients, but there is a tendency for the patient to be fitted into the team's structure rather than having the team individualize its various ways of working with a specific patient. Each individual who deals with the patient should have his particular contribution worked out with the therapist so that specific supportive goals can be identified and the means to reach those goals elaborated.

"Psychotherapy" by house officers or other members of the team should be carefully coordinated with the goals that the principal therapist himself is working towards. Unfortunately, not infrequently on inpatient psychiatric wards the attending psychiatrist, who is treating a patient pharmacologically or with electroconvulsive therapy, requests a resident to "take care of the psychotherapy." The resident, usually in his first or second year, rarely understands just what kind of psychotherapy he should be doing or how he should be doing it. Except in the most unusual situations, and these generally involve patients in long-term residential treatment centers, most psychotherapy carried out with the hospitalized patient will be primarily of the supportive type. Unless the resident has some concept of what he is doing, his work will tend to be haphazard and of little benefit to the patient.

SUPPORT GROUPS FOR OUTPATIENTS

For outpatients myriad "support groups" are available. These may be organized along a variety of lines. There are groups of former psychiatric patients, alcohol or drug abusers, parents without partners, and groups of divorced or separated individuals; there are numerous women's groups and, more recently, groups of men; and there are groups of veterans suffering, for example, from a posttraumatic illness. There are groups of individuals with emotional problems whose common bond is some shared religious faith.

Some groups are less clearly supportive and may seek some degree of insight, such as groups of professionals who meet to discuss and explore the implications of their work and its effects on their psychological well-being. There is, of course, group therapy for a variety of individuals; the goals of these groups range from the development of insight to the most basic types of support—such as groups of schizophrenic patients who are in a state of remission. Physical illnesses, especially chronic conditions, also form the basis for many groups: individuals with terminal illness, colostomy and ileostomy patients, etc. Some groups are organized for the families of the patient, such as parents of autistic children or of children with cerebral palsy.

How does the support group give support? One of its chief functions seems to be that by bringing together people with similar problems it provides them with a form of nurturance or mothering that comes from the implicit and explicit communality of feelings that the members of the group share. One member can be empathic with another because he too experiences and understands only too well the problems of the other. At the same time, because he himself is likely to receive the empathic understanding of the others, he does not tend to feel drained. Unfortunately, this situation does not always work out in practice because the needs and self-soothing abilities of all the members of the group are not alike. A member of the group who feels especially deprived may feel entitled to an inordinately larger share of support from the group. Members with strong sadistic or masochistic tendencies will also tend to use the group for their own needs. If the group is guided by a competent leader, gross inequalities between the group participants can be managed. But if there is no competent leader and no member emerges who has the ability to channel disruptiveness into useful channels, the group can become more destructive than supportive.

A second important function of the group is that it has the potential to support reality testing, which often means challenging distortions of reality put forward by a group member. Again, the group provides no guarantee that this will be done; groups, indeed entire nations, can share even crude distortions of reality. When that occurs, it actually reinforces the poor reality testing of the individual by giving it the stamp of consensual validation.

Because groups are miniature societies, they tend to foster socializing skills in their members. In order to obtain the approval and acceptance of the group, a member tends to discover that he must adapt, at least to some minimal extent, to the standards of the group. The group may have excessively high or low standards, which may be inappropriate for a given participant. If possible, this should be monitored by the leader so that no one patient is either subject to punitive rejection by the group or permitted total license.

The variety of "social" groups toward which a patient may be directed seems almost endless: groups by religious affiliation, athletic teams, hiking and camping groups, choral societies and musical ensembles, craft groups, etc., not to mention fraternal organizations, ethnic clubs, and community support groups.

WORK

Work is perhaps the most fruitful activity for the majority of people. It strengthens their self-esteem, fosters economic independence, serves as a powerful sublimation of sexual and aggressive drive impulses, and brings them into a community of similarly occupied individuals. Regular, gratifying and remunerative work is certainly the best sublimation for most people, but it is often either unavailable or the patient is not able to join the work force because of his longstanding emotional problems, his lack of expertise, or his poor work history.

Many communities have vocational rehabilitation services where the patient can be evaluated and perhaps directed to an appropriate technical school or to a center where he can receive on-the-job training. For some of the more severely disturbed patients, a sheltered workshop can be ideal; unfortunately, the number of such centers is sorely limited. However, a business firm will sometimes be willing to hire an individual to perform relatively undemanding work. Finally, in most communities there are opportunities for volunteer work in hospitals, nursing homes, day-care centers, schools, etc.

SPECIAL GROUPS

There are also special groups and centers that deal with specific psychological problems, and when such a disturbance is present the therapist should have access to a good resource file or to an individual with information about the available agencies. Alcoholics Anonymous, alcoholic rehabilitation centers, and drug treatment centers are typical of this type of supportive service, and their aid can be invaluable.

There are many groups that offer "psychotherapy" and promote a wide variety of treatments which are often only marginally related to mainstream group therapy. However, if the referring therapist is reasonably sure that the group in question is not likely to be actually destructive to the patient, and that it is being led by serious minded, dedicated individuals, it might be well to support the patient's interest in such an auxiliary form of "therapy," at least on a trial basis. Very often such groups support the defenses of intellectualization and rationalization by the explanations they give the patient for his behavior. Self-help books, whose number is legion, are also able to work in this manner. It is my impression that many of the improvements that result from these modalities last only for a relatively limited time, and the patient goes on to another therapy fad. However, if this helps provide support to the patient, in the ways outlined here, I can see no objection.

MEDICATION

One of the most powerful auxiliary measures in supportive work today consists of the arsenal of psychotropic drugs. The utility, indeed the necessity, of prescribing medication for certain patients is generally agreed upon by almost all mental health professionals. Patients suffering from manic-depressive illness, endogenous depression, schizophrenia, and nonspecific psychoses will almost always benefit from appropriate medication. Lithium, the neuroleptics, and several groups of antidepressant drugs are effective and fairly specific.

To prescribe a given medication does not necessarily imply that the patient must continue to take it indefinitely. When the patient has attained some level of equilibrium, the therapist can consider diminishing the dose and eventually stopping the medication altogether. In selected cases, it may prove useful to keep the patient on a maintenance dose indefinitely. With still other patients, it may become necessary to change medication when the product used is no longer efficacious.

The physician-therapist not only should be knowledgeable about the possible side effects of the drugs he prescribes, but should realize that these medications may lead to unusual and frightening feelings in the patient who is usually unprepared for such reactions. There is no point in telling the patient about every possible side effect of the drug which has been prescribed for him, but he should be told that there are some *common* side effects, such as dryness of the mouth or sleepiness; this is usually reassuring. He should also be told that he must promptly call the therapist if he experiences any other disturbing side effects.

Many psychotherapists are not physicians and may be unfamiliar with psychotropic drugs; in any event they are not permitted to prescribe them. But the established value of these medications makes it incumbent upon the nonmedical therapist to familiarize himself with them and the indications for their usage. He ought to recognize when psychotropic medication is indicated and refer the patient to a physician. He should also be aware of their side effects because he may be working with patients who are taking medication, and they may report symptoms which represent untoward reactions.

Since the non-physician-therapist himself cannot prescribe medication, and must call upon a physician, usually a psychiatrist, to do so, the relationship between them can at times become confused, adversarial, and thus eventually harmful to the patient's welfare. When a patient is referred to a psychiatrist for medication, he should be carefully evaluated in order to establish if there is a need for medication. Moreover, if the psychiatrist does not continue to see the patient in psychotherapy, he should maintain a frequency of contact with the patient which is appropriate to the particular medication prescribed. Collaboration between the therapist and the psychiatrist generally need not include all the details of the therapist's work with the patient other than those facts which bear on the indications for medication.

When psychotropic medication is prescribed, it is useful to re-member that along with the specific activity of a product there is a placebo effect which should be utilized. In fact, a medication can be prescribed in such a diffident and skeptical way as to have a *negative* placebo effect. If a drug is to be prescribed, the patient should understand that he is being given a powerful, specific product which has a high probability of leading to at least some and even considerable improvement in his symptoms. The prob-lem of compliance, the actual taking of the medication, is a difficult and important one, and the therapist should be aware that the best assurance that the patient is cooperating in taking his med-ication as prescribed lies in the firmness of the therapeutic rela-tionship between the patient and him. This involves issues of trust, the therapist's unfailingly supportive attitude, his empathy, and the patient's grasp of reality.

"NEGATIVE" INFLUENCES

Finally, there are "negative forms" of support in that the ther-apist tries to isolate the patient from individuals or situations which have been repeatedly demonstrated to be "toxic" for him. As mentioned earlier, it is very helpful for the patient to learn what is injurious to him as well as what helps him. This is usually a slow process, requiring repeated confrontations, clarifications, and many painful experiences before the patient is able to put into practice what he has learned intellectually.

One aspect of this problem relates to the environment of the patient. At times it becomes painfully obvious that it is in the patient's best interest, for example, for him to leave his family, and even he may be keenly aware of that necessity. Nevertheless, it is often very difficult for these patients to sever, even if only partially, their dependent ties to their family. The therapist can only work towards this goal little by little, and then only if the patient at least accepts the principle of separating from his family.

A therapist who works with patients in supportive therapy soon learns that his desire for quick results not only will be frustrated, but as in all psychotherapy, "pushing" the patient is destructive of the therapeutic relationship, chiefly because it demonstrates to the patient that the therapist has not been really empathically following him but has, rather, been following his own idea of how things should be progressing and at what tempo. No matter how regressed a patient is, he usually remains capable of recognizing if the therapist is genuinely responsive to him. It cannot be repeated too often in all psychotherapeutic work, but perhaps more often in supportive psychotherapy than in other modalities, that the twin guidelines of empathy and flexibility are the foundation of treatment.

17

Termination and Interruption

A major difference between supportive psychotherapy and insight-oriented psychotherapy lies in their respective approaches to the question of termination. Indeed, the very concept, when used in the sense of a *therapeutic* termination, is frequently inappropriate in supportive psychotherapy, and it is generally more useful to think in terms of interruption. Viewed somewhat schematically, the typical patient in supportive psychotherapy, as he has been described, is an individual whose psychological difficulties stem rather more from insufficiencies or deficits in various ego functions than from conflicts between drive impulses and the prohibitions against them.

PROGRESS TO INSIGHT-ORIENTED PSYCHOTHERAPY

To the extent that this typical patient in supportive psychotherapy actually has undergone some degree of ego development, we can say that there has been sufficient enhancement of those formerly limited ego functions to permit him to work in a more insight-oriented mode of treatment. Then, depending on the patient's needs and wishes, therapy may progressively take on the characteristics of explorative work, as described more fully in Chapter XV.

Mrs. Annette M., a 40-year-old separated receptionist, came for help because she "couldn't get along with people" and felt sad and angry much of the time. She was suspicious, chronically angry and, though she did not acknowledge it, manifestly frightened by closeness with other people. Her frequent use of projection and splitting made her often appear to be living in a quasi-delusional world. Her rage surrounded her like a barbed wire fence, and therapy hours consisted of diatribes directed, at one time or another, against almost everyone in her environment. Mrs. M.'s therapist was often the unhappy recipient of her attacks, particularly when he attempted to confront her with *her* part in the disputes she reported.

After about three years of mostly supportive work with weekly visits, it became evident that there had been a qualitative change in the frequency and intensity of these fights with her therapist. One day, after the patient had sarcastically called him a "great Samaritan," she stopped and excused herself, saying, "This time I had no cause to get on your back. I don't know why I always seem to poor-mouth you. You've never missed an hour and you've always been decent to me." The therapist replied, "Sometimes a person will insult another as a way of convincing himself that he doesn't care about that person. Maybe that's one reason why you often get on my back." Mrs. M. remained thoughtful for a while and finally said, "I don't think it was that way at first. In the beginning, I really thought you *were* like everyone else, that you thought I was a nut. But somewhere along the line I found that I was looking forward to coming here. I even began to enjoy my visits at times. The other day I thought, 'The doctor is the only friend I ever had.' You know, I never felt my parents gave a damn about me." Gradually the therapist began to engage Mrs. M. in clarifying and looking at her thoughts, feelings, and behavior—less now in an effort to "correct" these than to help her understand them. Therapy increasingly tended to be explorative with some insight as a goal.

CONTINUING SUPPORT

In contrast, Miss Olivia R., a 23-year-old woman, was first seen when she was brought to the hospital emergency room after a suicide attempt following the breakup of a love affair. She stayed a month on a psychiatric inpatient service and was then discharged, followed by weekly sessions with the psychiatric resident who had been treating her there. Miss R. was an intelligent, verbal, attractive woman, and the therapist began psychotherapy with her, without ever having specifically defined for himself or the patient whether it was supportive or insight-oriented, or what his goals were. Treatment was aimed vaguely at developing some "growth."

The first difficulty was that Miss R. rarely had anything to say, and during the 15 months that her therapist saw her she was silent most of the time. The therapist tried everything he and his supervisor could think of. Little by little it became clear that Miss R. had already developed an erotic transference to her therapist when he was taking care of her during her hospitalization, and that it had become much stronger during her weekly outpatient visits. He repeatedly interpreted her silence as due to her embarrassment at telling him about her feelings for him, but with no response. After several months without apparent change in the therapeutic situation—but with considerable sexual acting-out of the transference with various men, the therapist decided to change the frequency of the patient's visits from once a week to twice a month because, he told her, "We really don't seem to have enough to talk about." That night, the patient cut her wrists superficially and was readmitted to the hospital.

Another resident, who was assigned to the inpatient service, began to follow Miss R. He was able to benefit from the former therapist's mistaken decision that the patient could benefit from insight-oriented psychotherapy, and after a three-day hospitalization, he agreed to see Miss R. as an outpatient. Thirty-minute visits were scheduled for twice a month, with the understanding that they would aim at even less frequent interviews once she settled down in her new job.

Although the patient at first protested at the infrequency, she finally agreed. After a few months, visits were reduced to once a month, and at the end of the year scheduled visits were given up altogether. The patient and the therapist agreed that she would come to the outpatient clinic when she wanted help with a specific problem. At first she came every few weeks and was seen as a "walk-in" patient by whichever staff member was available. In this way, she formed no ongoing close contact with any one individual. Her visits grew more infrequent but she still appeared about two or three times a year. She seemed to have become firmly but moderately attached to the clinic, which suggested that she had developed an "institutional transference."

This type of transference was described by Reider (1953) and is an excellent way of following some patients who are in supportive psychotherapy, since it helps avoid the intense transference reactions to a given therapist which the patient may not be able to tolerate and which cannot be properly worked through. Furthermore, in psychiatric clinics and mental health centers, the periodic turnover of staff who are there for training can be upsetting for many of the patients in the group under consideration. However, patients who develop an institutional transference usually expect that at the end of June they will be assigned to a new therapist, as their previous one moves on. Generally, they navigate this changeover with tolerable anxiety and a minimal grief reaction.

TERMINATION VS. INTERRUPTION

In light of the characteristics of the typical patient in supportive psychotherapy, it is clear why a "therapeutic termination" occurs infrequently in this mode of treatment. The patient is likely to maintain some contact, brief or infrequent as it may be, with the therapist (or clinic), or all visits cease—but this should more properly be regarded as an *interruption*, since it is very probable that sooner or later the patient will return, usually in the midst of a crisis.

Although this might well be said about many patients who have been in insight-oriented psychotherapy, when termination occurs there, one is more likely to have observed some objective progress in terms of reduction of conflict or modifications in character. In contrast, a realistic goal for a patient in supportive psychotherapy is to help them reach some reasonable psychological and adaptational equilibrium. They will have, in effect, more or less reached the maximum of their potential regarding work (or school), relations with the people who are close to them, obligations and responsibilities to society, and feelings of inner harmony. Such an equilibrium may never be reached, or may be maintained only for short periods of time—spells of good function punctuated by more or less frequent crises. For such patients, interruption is generally not advisable; some contact, even if it be only every two or three months, is preferable.

It might be said that such a suggestion is tantamount to saying that supportive psychotherapy should continue indefinitely for some patients. Indeed, that is what is indicated for some individuals. The analogy with patients with such incurable illnesses as diabetes or essential hypertension is appropriate here. The patient and his illness cannot be fundamentally altered, but good management can prevent intercurrent illness and premature death.

It is often not clear just what path to take in regard to interruption because the patient may demonstrate markedly erratic behavior. There is no way to handle this difficulty other than by trial and error. As a general rule, the less the patient needs to see the therapist, the better. Less contact generally fosters autonomy and tacitly encourages the patient to try and work out his problems by himself or with the help of people in his environment. Of course, there is no special virtue attached to not seeing a therapist or to continuing doing so: there is only what is useful and indicated. In this regard, as discussed previously, interruptions can be made longer and can be formalized if the patient has learned to recognize early changes that suggest that psychological trouble is brewing, to avoid unhealthy situations, and to engage in ego-supportive activities.

Each time the patient returns after an interruption, the therapist should carefully review with him the months preceding the relapse, so that the patient may enrich his understanding of how those current difficulties developed. The therapist must be careful not to let the patient feel that he has "erred" in any manner, or that he has shamefully or stupidly brought these latest difficulties on himself. Such an attitude, aside from being inappropriate and hurtful, will only make the patient less likely to return promptly to the therapist the next time he is experiencing difficulties. Furthermore, most of these patients have sufficient problems with self-regard not to have to deal with the additional burden of humiliation or guilt fostered by the therapist. It may be true that the patient often has had some responsibility for the relapse, but that is something that can be explored later in a nonjudgmental, compassionate way, where the focus is clearly on clarifying and understanding.

It may be objected that to maintain an ongoing contact with a patient in supportive psychotherapy, no matter how infrequent the visits are, will foster an unremitting dependency in the patient, a situation that may become agreeable not only to him, if it was not so from the outset, but also to the therapist. Assuredly, more dependence on the therapist than the patient truly requires is not in the patient's best interests. Equally, it is not useful to deprive the patient of those "supplies" which he specifically requires and cannot fully obtain by himself. There is nothing gained in demanding of a patient that he do what is simply beyond his ability. To find the right level of expectation is difficult, and as with interruption generally, it often comes down to a matter of carefully tailoring one's approach to each patient's needs.

One particular and frequent situation occurs with a patient who initially comes or is brought to a therapist because of an acute crisis. When the major manifestations of the crisis have abated, most such patients are perfectly happy to stop seeing the therapist. In these situations it is useful to encourage the patient to continue to come for further interviews, especially when the emotional upheaval has subsided and he is better able to look with more detachment on what provoked the crisis. If, as so typically happens, the patient no longer wishes treatment, he should be encouraged to return promptly in the future if and when he sees the same developments occurring.

Epilogue

This book is based on the premise that when supportive psychotherapy can be a coherent, organized endeavor that it can be helpful to large numbers of patients and be gratifying to the psychotherapist.

As the reader will have seen, my focus has been on helping the patient rather than on an adherence to inviolate rules or theoretical assumptions. Theory, as Freud wrote, is but a scaffolding—subject to change and even liable to be torn down and replaced. If theory usefully informs practice, it is of worth; when it impedes practice, it is nothing but a millstone.

Moreover, nothing advances theory better than putting it to the test. In my experience, the psychoanalytic concepts I have drawn on for guidance in practicing supportive psychotherapy have been effective. However, the therapist should be attuned to new developments in a field which, for better and for worse, has been mushrooming with new approaches.

More fundamental perhaps, than matters of theory and technique, is the attitude of the psychotherapist about his patient. Regardless of theoretical persuasion or technical modality, I believe that respect for the patient must be the *sine qua non* of all psychotherapeutic work. The most regressed, bizarre, or intractable patient is no less deserving of the therapist's concern and respect than any other patient. Compassion and empathy and a nonjudgmental attitude should pervade all psychotherapeutic work. There are many ways to be in the world—some quite alien to us—and the therapist should be prepared to accept his patient's path as long as it is not harmful to the patient or to others. The therapist's role is to help the patient become as much like the person he wants to be as is possible, and if the therapist cannot accept the patient's goals he should disqualify himself from his task as helper.

It is an everlasting problem to find the correct path to follow between excessive expectations of a patient and a nihilistic position that expects nothing of him. For this there are no simple guidelines other than a constant awareness of the problem and an attempt to see clearly how the patient is responding to the treatment process. Many of the patients seen in supportive psychotherapy are sufficiently disturbed for the therapist to be truly gratified with even small steps forward. The effects of such modest changes may prove to be much greater than one had anticipated. Additionally, these improvements may lead to responses from the people in the patient's environment that can further enhance his inner harmony and his adaptation to the external world.

Practicing supportive psychotherapy is a notable endeavor. Everyone who does this work should feel gratified with the contribution he is making; there is no more worthy effort than to help relieve a little human misery.

References

Asch, S. S. Varieties of negative therapeutic reaction and problems of technique. *Journal of the American Psychoanalytic Association*, 1976, 24:383-407.

Beck, A. T., Rush, A. J., Shaw, B. F. et al. *Cognitive therapy of depression.* New York: Guilford Publications, 1979.

Bibring, E. The mechanism of depression. In P. Greenacre (Ed.), *Affective disorders.* New York: International Universities Press, 1953.

Bibring, E. Psychoanalysis and the dynamic psychotherapies. *Journal of the American Psychoanalytic Association*, 1954, 2:745-770.

Brenner, C. The masochistic character: Genesis and treatment. *Journal of the American Psychoanalytic Association*, 1959, 7:197-226.

Brenner, C. *An elementary textbook of psychoanalysis* (rev. ed.). New York: Anchor Books, 1974.

Breuer, J. & Freud, S. Studies in hysteria, *Complete Psychological Works*, Vol. 2. London: Hogarth Press, 1952, 2:3-319.

Dewald, P. *Psychotherapy.* New York: Basic Books, 1964.

Feather, B. W. Psychodynamic behavior therapy: I. Theory and rationale. *Archives of General Psychiatry*, 1972, 26:496-502.

Feather, B. W. Psychodynamic behavior therapy: II Clinical aspects. *Archives of General Psychiatry*, 1972, 26:503-511.

Freud, S. (1915) Observations on transference love. *Standard Edition*, 12:158-171. London: Hogarth Press, 1952.

Freud, S. (1924) The economic problem of masochism. *Standard Edition*, 19:157-170. London: Hogarth Press, 1952.

Freud, S. (1937) Analysis terminal and interminable. *Standard Edition*, 23:209-254. London: Hogarth Press, 1952.

Kubie, L. S. The destructive potential of humor. *American Journal of Psychiatry*, 1971, 127:861-866.

Modell, A. The "holding environment" and the therapeutic action of psychoanalysis. *Journal of the American Psychoanalytic Association*, 1976, 24:285-307.

Pumpian-Mindlin, E. Comments on techniques of termination and transfer in a clinic setting. *American Journal of Psychotherapy*, 1958, 12:455-464.

Reider, N. A type of transference to institutions. *Bulletin of the Menninger Clinic,* 1953, 17:58-63.

Schafer, R. Talking to patients. *Bulletin of the Menninger Clinic,* 1974, 38:503-515.

Ullman, L. P. & Krasner, L. (Eds.). *Case studies in behavior modification.* New York: Holt, Rinehart and Winston, 1965.

Werman, D. S. The use of dreams in psychotherapy. *Canadian Psychiatric Association Journal,* 1978, 23:153-158.

Werman, D. S. Technical aspects of supportive psychotherapy. *Psychiatric Journal of the University of Ottawa,* 1981, 6:153-160.

Winnicott, D. W. Psychiatric disorders in terms of infantile maturational processes. In *The maturational process and the facilitating environment.* New York: International Universities Press, 1963.

Zetzel, E. R. The so-called good hysteric. *International Journal of Psycho-Analysis,* 1968, 49:256-260.

Index

187